Demystifying Spiritual Warfare

Luc Niebergall

Printed in the United States of America

First Edition, 2016

ISBN-13: 978-1530180639
ISBN-10: 1530180635

Royal Identity Ministries

Contents:

Introduction

One evening the Lord kept me awake throughout the night. As I sought His heart, Holy Spirit spoke to me very clearly saying that He wanted to release new things over my life, and that I was to partner with Him by doing a short fast. The very next morning as my wife was separately spending time with the Lord, Holy Spirit began to speak to her as well about starting a short fast. Together, we fasted from food for five days until we felt the Lord release us.

For many years, I have enjoyed taking drives with the Lord in the evenings. On these drives God will often speak to me, and they have become times where I often receive revelation from His heart. Shortly after our fast was complete, I was on one of these drives with the Lord. I felt the Spirit of Revelation come upon me in a much stronger way than usual. I immediately began to comprehend things concerning spiritual warfare that I had not understood before. Principles that were foreign to me became clear. Parallels and interpretations of certain scriptures were pieced together instantly in my heart. In the space of an hour long drive, Holy Spirit deposited the information and revelation for an entire book into my spirit. This revelation that I received is written in the book that you are now holding in your hands.

Just as the information in this book was supernaturally given to me, so too was the process of writing it. I have written and published several books, but this book has by far been the fastest that I have written to date. It only took me 10 days total to complete.

While writing this book, and for a time after completing it, I experienced intense spiritual warfare, some of which impacted my health. I know, without a doubt, that this was the enemy's attempt to try and prevent this book from being published. However, the enemy is under the feet of Jesus, and the Son of Man's works will forever be established no matter the opposition.

I believe that this book was given to me to better equip believers to understand the spirit realm and our part to play in advancing God's kingdom in the context of spiritual warfare.

Spiritual warfare is a topic that seems complex and it is often assumed that only some should be able to comprehend it. My heart is to both demystify and simplify the topic.

As we journey together throughout this book, my desire is that you will learn how to receive freedom from various forms of demonic torment, and how to receive healing in the realm of the soul. By giving both practical and spiritual tools, I will show you how to walk victoriously in body, soul and spirit. This way our entire being is brought under the reign of Jesus, instead of giving any form of foothold to the enemy.

Spiritual warfare should not look like us simply trying to survive through the battle. It should look like us understanding our royal identity, which means that we are seated above the battle. We have the opportunity and privilege of influencing the spiritual war that is taking place from a posture of rest, authority and victory.

Overcoming the enemy's tactics has little to do with battling; it has everything to do with abiding. It has everything to do with being.

The Origin of Spiritual Warfare

You are more important than you realize. You are so important that the Creator of the universe became a man so that your heart could be reconciled to His. He did this because He desires to be in relationship with you. You are so important that the Creator of the universe is continually advocating for you. He is endlessly paving a way for you to walk into your unique calling and destiny. He is committed to refining you; to training you. He does this because He takes you seriously and believes in your potential to step into greatness. All of God's great kingdom stands behind you in support, championing you onward as you understand who you were created to be.

When you are walking in your royal identity as a son or daughter of God, you forcefully advance the kingdom of God wherever you go. You were created to be a history maker and one who impacts eternity.

The effect of your importance does not just impact one kingdom. It does not just affect the kingdom of heaven by advancing its cause. You stepping into the fullness of who God has created you to be affects the kingdom of darkness by exposing its darkness and expelling it with the light of God's unmatched love. Since your understanding of who you were created to be affects both the kingdom of God and the kingdom of darkness, there is constant tension. There is a persistent advancement of God's kingdom sowing into you, to empower you. At the same time the kingdom of darkness is consistently trying to invade your life to reap what is not rightfully its own. We are in a constant war. This is a battle over your identity. One side says that you are an orphan, the other side says that you are a child of God. On one end, you are told that you are a peasant, on the other, you are declared as royalty. The kingdom of darkness tells you that you are a coward, yet the kingdom of heaven tells you that you were created to be a hero.

I have heard many teachings on spiritual warfare and have noticed that they often have a tendency to feel heavier and more complicated than they need to be. Although it is true that there is a battle taking place, Jesus' yoke is easy and His burden is light. My heart throughout this book is to guide you; to equip you with tools so that you would know how to fight this war from a place of victory. My desire is to take this seemingly elaborate concept of spiritual warfare, and demystify and simplify it. Something I have learned over the years is that the gospel is tremendously simple. It is simple because the core value of the kingdom of God is love. Everything in God's kingdom revolves around this core value. Topics such as spiritual warfare only become complicated when we try to wrap them up in worldly logic and extreme intellectualism.

In order to lay a basic foundation for you concerning spiritual warfare, I would like to walk with you through the verse that I believe reveals the origin of spiritual warfare.

In Genesis 3, satan comes in the appearance of a snake to tempt Eve to eat from the tree of the knowledge of good and evil. Eve then convinces Adam to give in to temptation just as she did. When God comes to pronounce the consequences of them choosing to eat from the forbidden tree, He first speaks to the enemy in Genesis 3:15. He says, "And I (God) will put enmity between you (satan) and the woman, and between your seed and her Seed; He shall bruise your head, and you shall bruise His heel." (NKJV)

Now, I really want to take time to unpack this verse with you, because this is much more profound than we think upon first glance. This verse lays out for us the foundation of spiritual warfare.

It is interesting that in this verse when God says He will put enmity between Eve's Seed and satan's seed, that Eve's 'Seed' is capitalized in the New King James Version Bible. When this type of noun is capitalized in the Bible and is not at the beginning of a sentence it is because it is not referring to a regular person, but is instead referring to God. Many scholars believe that this verse was referring to Christ. This verse is actually prophesying that God will be born from a woman. He will be her Seed. Even as far back as the fall of man, this verse prophesied that Christ would be born from the lineage of Adam and Eve. It prophesied that God would be born in the flesh. Right at that moment when mankind fell, God declared His action plan to redeem His children. This is the very first prophecy about Jesus coming to the earth in the Bible. The extraordinary thing about this prophecy is that it was not prophesied by a prophet or prophetess. This was prophesied by God Himself.

Are you intrigued yet? It gets much better. We need to look at the audience that God was prophesying to. God was not prophesying this to mankind; He was prophesying to the enemy. God was declaring that He was going to be born in the flesh, and would put enmity between Himself and satan. The word *enmity,* translated from the Hebrew, actually means 'hatred'. God did not say that enmity would simply exist between Him and satan, but that God Himself would be sure to put it there. Before God said this, the enemy had poked and prodded at God, but in this prophetic word, God was declaring war. Based on what we can see Biblically, this verse is the origin of spiritual warfare. Not only did God declare war, but He declared that He would be the victor. The enemy's head would be under His foot.

This is important for us to camp on. Many view spiritual warfare as though we are on the defence. We see warfare as though the enemy is attacking, and we need to learn to adjust to his tactics. We absolutely need to be aware of the enemy's schemes; however, the origin of spiritual warfare shows that God Himself was the one who initiated war. With Him, we are the ones on the offense who have the opportunity to partner with Him to destroy the works of darkness. We have the great honour of being part of the army of God, to partner with Christ to demolish the works of the kingdom of darkness with the kingdom of heaven. We have the privilege of being a part of this prophetic word in coming to pass.

Joel 2:11: "The Lord gives voice before His army, for His camp is very great."

Now, we need to ask ourselves a question: What was it that stirred God to such emotion to the point that He would wage warfare against the enemy? God waged warfare because satan attacked the most precious thing to His heart; His son and daughter, Adam and Eve. It is amazing how everything comes back to the Father heart of God. Everything always comes back to intimacy with Him.

If we are going to commit to destroying the works of the kingdom of darkness, then we need to do it from the standpoint from which spiritual warfare was initiated. If spiritual warfare was ignited by the Father heart of God, then we need to be rooted in a revelation of the Father's love for us in order to perceive spiritual warfare through a healthy lens. If we have a distorted image of God, believing that He initiated warfare simply because He was angry for no reason, we will miss the mark in spiritual warfare. God initiated spiritual warfare out of love for His children. It is when we have a proper perception of the Father heart of God, that we will truly see His kingdom established. This revelation comes with walking in intimacy and friendship with the Lord. It is our closeness to Him in this way that allows His heart to be formed and fashioned within us.

In the church we have in many ways forgotten the internal work of formation. We have believed that if we have new programs and create a proper external structure that people would reach spiritual maturity by being in our manmade wineskin. However, this is not the way that Jesus brought forth true sons and disciples. Jesus' disciples saw Him and in turn saw the Father. As they saw Christ and made Him their focus, Jesus began to be formed within them.

Exodus 33 explains how Moses and Joshua would spend time in the tent of meeting where the glory of the Lord dwelled. After some time passed Moses would depart and attend to His ministry duties, whereas Joshua would remain in the tent spending time with the Lord. After Moses died and Joshua was called to lead the Israelites into the Promised Land, Joshua had an encounter with the Lord that transitioned Him into walking into his greater calling.

Joshua 5:13-15: "And it came to pass, when Joshua was by Jericho, that he lifted his eyes and looked, and behold, a Man stood opposite him with His sword drawn in His hand. And Joshua went to Him and said to Him, 'Are You for us or for our adversaries?' So He said, 'No, but as Commander of the army of the Lord I have now come.' And Joshua fell on his face to the earth and worshiped, and said to Him, 'What does my Lord say to His servant?' Then the Commander of the Lord's army said to Joshua, 'Take your sandal off your foot, for the place where you stand is holy.' And Joshua did so."

Before Joshua could walk in his calling as a commander to lead Israel into the Promised Land, he needed to first know God the Leader and

Commander. As Joshua began to see and know Him, God the Commander began to be formed within him. This was crucial if Joshua was to step into his high calling. We need to be directly linked to God in friendship and intimacy if we are going to destroy the works of the enemy from a place of maturity. A true revelation of spiritual warfare will always come with knowing God the Commander personally. It comes with encountering His heart. From this place we are appropriately equipped to co-labour with Christ on the earth.

God is raising up a great army who is rooted in the secret place with Him. From this place of friendship with Him, the heart of God will be formed and fashioned within the inner man. This will give us the ability to war as representatives of the kingdom of heaven from a place of maturity and love.

About two years ago I was finishing up a school that I was teaching called, 'Experiencing the Glory of God'. While driving to the final evening of the class, Holy Spirit spoke to me saying, "Luc, when you get to the church I want you to head up to the upper room. I am going to meet you there." I was instantly excited considering that when God says He is going to meet with you, you know that something profound is going to happen.

When I arrived at the church, I headed upstairs to the upper room and popped in my headphones. As I worshipped God, a cloud of glory began to fill the room. This was not something that you needed to use your spiritual eyes to see by faith. There was a literal cloud in the natural that filled the room just as when the glory of God filled the temple in the Old Testament (2 Chronicles 5:14). Basking in the presence of Jesus, I took a seat on one of the chairs in the room when I was taken into an encounter.

I was suddenly taken into a heavenly encounter such as Paul mentioned in 2 Corinthians 12:2-4. The place that I was visiting in heaven was the heavenly courts (Daniel 7). Around me in the courtroom were hundreds of thousands of people. I discerned that these were different kingdom leaders from throughout the world who were believing for a global revival. I recognized a few of the leaders, since some were well known throughout the world. Each of us looked around to one another in wonder as to why we were summoned to this particular meeting in the courts of heaven.

Suddenly Jesus stepped onto the stage before us. He carried so much authority that His very presence demanded the silence of hundreds of thousands of leaders. He is indeed the King of kings. He stood quietly for a time. Then suddenly He reached behind His back and pulled something forth. What He now held out in front of us to see was a mantle. As thousands of eyes watched Him, Jesus spoke, saying, "This was the mantle of a great man of God who led thousands of people into the kingdom of God in his lifetime."

Jesus said his name, however, for the sake of honour and confidentiality I will keep his name private. Jesus went on sharing with us all of the great feats that this man had accomplished for the gospel while he was on the earth. He truly honoured the man. Then Jesus said something which caught us all off guard. He said, "Yet, this man only completed 80% of the ministry that I had laid out before Him."

When Jesus said this, everyone who listened held their breath, waiting for what Jesus was going to say next. Allowing silence to linger for a time, Jesus then completed what He wanted to say. He said, "The reason why this man only completed 80% of his ministry on the earth is because he had forgotten his first love. Since he did not put intimacy with the Godhead as his primary priority, he did not complete the mandate over his life."

Everyone looked at one another, wondering why Jesus was sharing information such as this. Jesus then continued, "Since my word cannot come back void, who here is willing to pick up this mantle to complete his mandate?" Silence reigned in the atmosphere for a time, when a woman stepped up to the stage and allowed Jesus to place the mantle on her shoulders. When she left the stage, Jesus pulled another mantle out from behind

His back. He said, "This was the mantle of a great woman of God, who led hundreds into the kingdom in her lifetime. Yet, she only completed 20% of her ministry because she forgot her first love. My word cannot come back void, so who will pick up her mantle?" We waited again in silence until someone came up to take on the incomplete mandate. Jesus did this with dozens of mantles throughout the course of this meeting.

When my encounter was finished, I was back in the upper room, still enshrouded in the cloud of glory. Holy Spirit then spoke to me saying, "The most important test that any believer will face in their lifetime is this question, 'Do you remember your first love?'"

God is raising up a generation whose greatest desire will be to know Him. He is calling His people Into the secret place to walk in intimacy with Him. Friendship with God is the greatest level of ministry, and God is looking for those who will first and foremost pursue the deep things of His heart. We are living in amazing times, where God is birthing a revival throughout the nations like never before. More signs, wonders, miracles and salvations are happening now than ever throughout the entire course of history. The only way for us to steward this move of God that is sweeping the earth globally is for us to prioritize our friendship with God above all else. This is where true love filled authority is forged. It is forged in the face to face encounters with the living

God.

We live amidst a spiritual battle. There is indeed a war taking place. It is a war which was birthed by love from the Father towards His children. We play a key part in this battle. We get to co-labour alongside of God in wielding the kingdom of heaven to demolish the kingdom of darkness. We get to do this out of a love for God's children that they will be reconciled back to the Father heart of God. In order to do this, we need to have our priorities set straight. We need to allow Jesus the Commander to be formed within us. We need to allow the heart of God the Father to take root in the deepest parts of our beings. We need to remember our first love, to be transformed into His likeness, in His embrace.

You are called by God to take a stand for truth and love. You are part of a great army, ordained to expand the dominion of the kingdom of God on the earth. You are chosen and marked to be a wielder of the kingdom of light.

In and with Christ, you are the victor.

The Invisible Realm

2 Corinthians 4:18: "So we fix our eyes not on what is seen, but on what is unseen, since what is seen is temporary, but what is unseen is eternal."

Before we dive into the intricacies concerning spiritual warfare, we need to be at a place where we are willing to put faith in the fact that there is indeed a spirit realm. Many in the church view the spiritual battle occurring around us as a metaphor. This is a dangerous assumption to make, considering that embracing such a belief would force us to disregard a vast portion of scripture. Not only do we need to understand that there is a spirit realm, but we need to understand that it is directly connected to the physical realm that we can see, hear, touch, taste and smell. In fact, the spirit realm directly influences the natural. In present times we often have a tendency to dismiss what we cannot discern with our natural senses. We brand concepts that are supernatural as fables, simply because they do not fit into our intellectual grid. However, placing our beliefs on what is logical is a dire mistake considering that we should be building our faith upon what the Word of God says and on what the Spirit testifies is true. The scriptures are filled with accounts of real people experiencing the supernatural and the spirit realm around them.

2 Kings 6:15-17: "When the servant of the man of God arose early and went out, there was an army, surrounding the city with horses and chariots. And his servant said to him, 'Alas, my master! What shall we do?' So he answered, 'Do not fear, for those who are with us are more than those who are with them.' And Elisha prayed, and said, 'LORD, I pray, open his eyes that he may see.' Then the LORD opened the eyes of the young man, and he saw. And behold, the mountain was full of horses and chariots of fire all around Elisha."

It is interesting to me that the servant in this passage was a different servant than Gehazi, who was Elisha's appointed apprentice. *Gehazi* translated in Hebrew means 'valley of vision', which means 'one who cannot see or perceive'. I believe that we are living in a time where God is delivering the church from an unwillingness to see and perceive the supernatural realm around us. He is giving us vision like Elisha's new servant to perceive the war that is taking place around us. This should not strike fear into your heart. When Elisha and his servant saw the army of God encamped around them, it did not give them strife or anxiety, but gave them courage because they were seeing the strategy of the Lord.

I will share a testimony with you to broaden your understanding of how what we are perceiving in the spirit realm can actually reveal to us the strategy of the Lord. A while ago I was getting lunch at a restaurant. As I was eating, I looked to the empty table beside me. When I looked, I began perceiving what was occurring in the spirit realm in this restaurant. I saw two angels with small wings preparing something at the table. When I see something in the spirit realm, I like to ask the Lord questions about what I am seeing to gain clarity.

When I consulted Holy Spirit, He spoke to me saying, "Those angels are preparing for someone's salvation. She will be arriving shortly." Immediately after Holy Spirit spoke that to me, a married couple walked into the restaurant and sat down at a table on the other side of the room.

When I saw the woman with her husband, I immediately felt like the Lord had given me a prophetic word for her and knew that she was the person who I was to minister to. I said to God, "I will give her a word, but I need You to bring her to the table where the angels were preparing for her salvation." At once, the woman stood up with her husband and they walked to the table beside me where the angels were.

I began overhearing their conversation and realized that they did not speak a word of English. I walked up to the married couple and double checked by saying, "Hi there, do you speak English?"

The response I received were two blank and confused stares. I figured that I would give her the prophetic word in spite of the language barrier, by faith, because spirit connects to spirit.

As I spoke the word to the woman, even though she could not understand a word I was saying, she began to openly weep and had a powerful encounter with Jesus right there in the restaurant.

We can see how what was happening in the realm of the spirit was something that God had used to directly influence the natural realm. Not only did God use it to impact this woman, but it was the very thing that God used to reveal His strategy to me so that He could touch her heart.

If we could only fully tap into the realm of the spirit, we would understand that there is a lot more taking place than we know. I stumbled across an interesting parallel in scripture that describes how one scenario looks in both the natural and spiritual realms. Look at this with me:

Luke 2:16-20: "They (the wise men) came with haste and found Mary and Joseph, and the Babe lying in a manger. Now when they had seen Him (Jesus), they made widely known the saying which was told them concerning this Child. And all those who heard it marvelled at those things which were told them by the shepherds. But Mary kept all these things and pondered them in her heart. Then the shepherds returned, glorifying and praising God for all the things that they had heard and seen, as it was told them."

The book of Revelation primarily focuses on future events; however, some of John's revelations and visions were referring to the present occurrences of that time as well as past events. Many overlook this, but in Revelation 12 it paints a picture for us of what it looked like in the spirit realm when Jesus was born.

Revelation 12:1-7: "Now a great sign appeared in heaven: a woman clothed with the sun, with the moon under her feet, and on her head a garland of twelve stars. Then being with child, she cried out in labor and in pain to give birth. And another sign appeared in heaven: behold, a great, fiery red dragon having seven heads and ten horns, and seven diadems on his heads. His tail drew a third of the stars of heaven and threw them to the earth. And the dragon stood before the woman who was ready to give birth, to devour her Child as soon as it was born. She bore a male Child who was to rule all nations with a rod of iron. And her

27

Child was caught up to God and His throne. Then the woman fled into the wilderness, where she has a place prepared by God, that they should feed her there one thousand two hundred and sixty days."

This is remarkable to me. I do not recall seeing a fiery red dragon with seven heads in any nativity scene. In this verse it shows us "a woman clothed with the sun, with the moon under her feet, and on her head a garland of twelve stars." I can assume that this is what Mary looked like in the spirit realm, since the story goes on to read that she was led into the wilderness for 1,260 days. This would make sense because after Jesus was born in Bethlehem, Joseph was instructed by an angel in a dream to take Mary and Jesus to Egypt so that King Herod would not kill the Son of Man. The three stayed in Egypt until Herod's death, which would have taken place about three and a half years (1,260 days) after Jesus' birth. This verse even shows us what it looked like in the spirit realm when satan (the dragon) took one third of the angels (stars) to earth with him. It is incredible what takes place in the spirit realm without us knowing it.

Angels

Acts 8:26: "Now an angel of the Lord spoke to Philip, saying, 'Arise and go toward the south along the road which goes down from Jerusalem to Gaza.'"

Angels are a very prominent component to what occurs in the spirit realm. Some people become uncomfortable when I talk about the angelic realm, but the truth is that God still uses angels to speak and minister to the saints. Angels are a part of God's kingdom. We do not get uncomfortable with teachings concerning other aspects of God's kingdom such as peace and joy, so we should not be offended by the angelic. In fact, to not believe in angels and in their interaction with mankind is tremendously unbiblical considering how frequently angels are mentioned in scripture.

Hebrews 1:14 says, "Are they (angels) not all ministering spirits sent forth to minister to those who will inherit salvation?" Do you know what this means? This means that whether you believe it or not, there are angels assigned to your life to minister to you. Not only are there angels assigned to your life, but there are more than likely angels around you in the spirit realm right now as you are reading this book.

Let me share a story with you to build your faith:

One time while I was teaching a course on the prophetic ministry at a church, I began sharing testimonies about different angelic encounters I have had. As I shared, I was watching those who were listening, when I began to see the pastor's wife quickly shuffling down one of the pews. The look on her face told me that she was a bit shaken up. I honestly had no clue what she was doing, so I continued teaching.

At the end of the service, the pastor's wife came and told me that when she was listening to my testimonies, she had asked God to see an angel. Immediately after she prayed her prayer, she heard something behind her. She turned and saw an angel walk into the sanctuary and it sat down right beside her on the pew. She started shuffling down the pew, because she was freaked out. When she finally sat still, the angel spoke to her a message from the Lord.

There are numerous accounts of angels in the Bible, most of which involve interactions with mankind. In many instances, whenever there was something profound taking place in scripture, angels were mentioned.

Remember the story of Peter's miraculous

escape from prison (Acts 12). Peter leaves the jail and goes to the house where the other believers are praying for his escape. When he knocks on the door, a young girl named Rhoda comes, hears his voice and runs to tell the others that Peter escaped. Now, notice the believer's response: they said to her, "You are beside yourself... It is his angel" and then they go back to praying for Peter's escape. Let me point something out here. They believe that this is a physical manifestation of an angel knocking at their door and talking to a young girl, yet they brush it off flippantly as if it is not a big deal. This is how normal it was for the early church to experience God moving through angels. If the saints of old have died then who else will they minister to other than you and me?

In Matthew 4:11, after Jesus was tempted by satan in the desert, it says, "then the devil left Him, and behold, angels came and ministered to Him." If Jesus the Messiah needed angels to minister to Him, then we definitely need to be humble enough to receive their ministry.

I believe there are many different types of angels. Considering the vast amount of angelic references in the Bible and the diversity of their ministry towards mankind, this must be a true statement. We are quick to believe that there are demons (spirits) of lust, poverty and anger. It only makes sense then that there would also be angels of purity, blessing and joy. If we believe that one third of the angels fell with satan, then there are

31

actually twice as many angels as there are demons (Revelation 12:4). John 5 mentions a healing angel that would stir the pool of Bethesda and whoever was the first to jump in the pool after it was stirred would be healed from any pain or infirmity. Most Biblical references of angels describe them as taking the form of males (Judges 13:6, Daniel 10:5-21); however Zechariah 5:5-9 mentions two angels who were in the form of women with wings like storks.

Here are some Biblical references to angelic encounters to boost your faith:

- Genesis 16:7-15
- Judges 6:11-22
- 1 Kings 19:5-8
- 1 Chronicles 21:9-27
- Zechariah 1:11-14
- Luke 1:26-38
- Acts 10:3-22
- Acts 12:7-11
- Acts 27:23
- Revelation 2, 3

I could go on for hundreds of pages unpacking scripture and sharing testimonies about the spiritual realm and how it surrounds us every moment of every day. However, it is hardly possible to read a story in scripture and not read about a supernatural reality invading the lives of normal men and women. Therefore, I will leave it to you to begin reading your Bible from a perspective that allows you to perceive the realm of the spirit through the Word of God. There is indeed a spirit realm, and like it or not, you are pivotal in the war that occurs around you day and night.

To end off the chapter, I would like to take time to lead you in a moment of prayer and perhaps, repentance. The reason why I say repentance, is that many of us either consciously or subconsciously have denied the fact that God is doing things greater than we can perceive in the natural realm. Many of us have dismissed the invisible spiritual realm purely because our intellect cannot understand it. We need to be willing to receive everything that God has for us. A time of repentance does not have to be long and drawn out. To repent simply means to change the way that you think. We all need to grow in the fullness of what God has to offer, so I will be praying as well as I write. If you want God to begin to open your awareness concerning what is occurring in the spirit realm, I encourage you to pray this with me:

"Holy Spirit, I repent for the times when I have dismissed what You are doing in the invisible realm. I repent for extreme intellectualism. Help me to shift my eyes to the unseen. I believe that there is a realm of the spirit. I believe that I have a part to play in what You are doing in the heavens. Train me in the ways of the Spirit. Activate my spiritual senses, Lord. Give me eyes to see and

ears to hear. Give me discernment that I may understand what You are doing in the unseen realm and that I may understand Your heavenly strategy."

Shifting from Fear to Authority

In the kingdom of God, your identity has more to do with being royalty than it does with being warrior-like. This is a foundational truth necessary for us to understand while discussing spiritual warfare. Once understood, this one revelation shifts us from a mentality of trying to survive in a war, to directly influencing the war for the kingdom of God.

Ephesians 6:12: "For we do not wrestle against flesh and blood, but against principalities, against powers, against the rulers of the darkness of this age, against spiritual *hosts* of wickedness in the heavenly places."

In this verse we clearly see that there is a battle taking place. If we were to try to visualize this verse, we would likely see ourselves fighting vigorously against spiritual beings. However, we cannot interpret the scriptures by leaning on our own understanding. Remember, our battle is not against flesh and blood, so therefore we will not wrestle with spiritual beings as though they were. Since it is a battle in the spirit realm, there are spiritual principals and tools that we are to use in this battle. We are not called to wrestle demonic spirits as though they are equals to us, because they are not. The demonic realm is not on the same playing field as we are. Through Christ, they are far below us in spiritual hierarchy.

A few years ago, a friend and I were in a coffee shop. As I was buying a coffee, two people caught my eye. They were sitting at a table with tarot cards scattered all over it. It was obvious that one of the women was a psychic in the middle of a tarot card reading, which she was performing for the other woman sitting across from her.

I then felt Holy Spirit drawing my attention to a man sitting next to the two women, and felt led to pray for him. I walked over, introduced myself and began to speak prophetically into his life. As I did this it opened the door for me to also pray over him. While my hand was on his shoulder, I prayed that God would touch his heart and life. All of a sudden, this man, who did not know God, began to feel the presence of God which spilled over in uncontrollable laughter. While he laughed, he began shouting out, thanking God for touching his heart. I find it comical when Holy Spirit chooses not to be discreet.

As I looked over to the table next to me, my eyes met the gaze of the psychic, who was clearly not pleased with me. I heard her beginning to mutter to the woman sitting across from her saying, "Ever since that man came near us, I haven't been able to read your fortune."

The psychic then stood up angrily, cast me a final angry glare and then stormed out of the coffee shop. Since the woman who was doing tarot card reading had left, this gave space for me to go minister prophetically to the woman who was formerly being spoken into by the psychic.

When this woman was operating in the occult, the kingdom of darkness was in fruition. Yet, when I went up to them, I carried the culture of God and the kingdom of heaven with me. There was warfare taking place in the spirit realm because two kingdoms were colliding. The reason why her psychic link was cut, preventing her from tarot card reading, was because the kingdom of God is far above the kingdom of darkness in spiritual hierarchy. There is no comparison in power. When the kingdom of God shows up, the kingdom of darkness is abolished. Many of us, when we see someone operating in things of the occult or see forms of demonic activity, we step into a mentality of fear, as though the kingdom of darkness is going to affect us in a negative way. We need to understand that in the kingdom of God you are never on the defense, but on the offense. We are called to be a light in the darkness. How are we supposed to be light if we are afraid of the dark? You should not be worried about the darkness getting on you, you should be focused on getting the light on them.

I am going to lay out some theology that will help you recognize your spiritual standing. To understand the spirit realm, we are going to look at the different heavens that the Bible refers to, and discuss our function in each.

2 Corinthians 12:1-4: "It is doubtless not profitable for me to boast. I will come to visions and revelations of the Lord: I know a man in Christ who fourteen years ago – whether in the body I do not know, or whether out of the body I do not know, God knows – such a one was caught up to the third heaven. And I know such a man – whether in the body or out of the body I do not know, God knows – how he was caught up into paradise and heard inexpressible words, which is not lawful for a man to utter."

Paul, in his letter to the Corinthians, mentions that he once knew a man who was caught up into the third heaven. Now, if there is a third heaven, then we need to assume that there is also a first and second heaven. Before God expanded my imagination, I pictured heaven to be a small place - maybe as big as a city or even a small country. However, I have learned that heaven is a wonderfully vast place. The first verse of the Bible, Genesis 1:1 says, "In the beginning God created the heavens and the earth." Notice how the word 'heavens' in this verse is plural where 'Earth' is not. Even the size of earth cannot compare to the enormity of heaven.

Most theologians will agree that the first heaven is the solar system. If you look at the creation account in Genesis 1:7 it talks about something called a 'firmament', which God named 'Heaven'. In verses 14-19 it talks about how the firmament is where the sun, moon and stars are. It could also easily be debated that because the firmament is a part of the natural realm, that all of the realm we see with our natural eyes is the first heaven.

The second heaven is what I believe the apostle Paul referred to in Ephesians 6:12: "For we do not wrestle against flesh and blood, but against principalities, against powers, against the rulers of the darkness of this age, against spiritual hosts of wickedness in the heavenly places." This verse shows us that Paul considered the spiritual realm where angels and demons battle, to be part of heaven.

The third heaven is a dimension away from the first heaven and above the second heaven where angels and demons battle. It is the place in heaven where God's throne is, where the streets of gold are and where the mansions of the saints have been built. The third heaven is the place that is spoken about in chapters like Isaiah 6, Ezekiel 1 and Revelation 4.

We know that we exist here on the earth in the natural realm, which we could refer to as the 'first heaven'. Psalm 115:16 says, "The heaven, even the heavens, are the Lord's; But the earth He has given to the children of men." The earth has been given to us by God to steward. Our job is to co-labour with Him to bridge His kingdom to earth.

One of the reasons why we have so much fear concerning the spirit realm is that we believe we are positioned in the second heaven where angels and demons battle. We need to understand that we are not seated there. It is not the place we are called to war from. We are called to war from the third heaven, where we are seated in Christ. Ephesians 2:6 says, "(Jesus) raised us up together, and made us sit together in the heavenly places in Christ Jesus."

When we believe that we are positioned in the second heaven, we take on a warrior mentality. We end up believing that we are on the same playing field as angels and demons, when in actuality, we are seated above the war that is taking place. We reign with Christ on His throne above the angels and demons (Revelation 3:21). We are not supposed to slip into a ground warfare mentality, but are called to see the battle from an aerial perspective as kings and queens of heaven, under the leadership of Christ. This is why there should be no fear in your heart concerning the spirit realm.

I have heard some argue that this cannot be true because Psalm 8:4-5 says, "What is man that you are mindful of him, and the son of man that you visit him, for You have made him a little lower than the angels." They believe that angels are actually greater and higher than us, making us even lower in authority than anything that exists in the second heaven. However, if we interpret this verse from the original language from which it was written, it says something quite different. The Hebrew word for 'angels' in this verse is *Elohim,* which means 'God'. This means that this verse should be read as, "What is man that you are mindful of him, and the son of man that you visit him, for You have made him a little lower than God." The same God who spoke the earth into existence, who created the planets, stars and galaxies, created us in His image a little lower than Himself. In spiritual hierarchy, you are in a higher place of authority than even the angels.

Let us take another look at Genesis 3:15

since there is more for us to unpack from it: "And I will put enmity between you and the woman, and between your seed and her Seed; He shall bruise your head, and you shall bruise His heel."

We discovered earlier that this verse was where spiritual warfare originated, and that the woman's seed refers to Jesus. This verse says that there will be enmity between Christ and satan's seed. So what would be satan's seed? Satan's seed refers to the works of the enemy and the kingdom that he reigns over, the kingdom of darkness. The fact that this verse says that Jesus will bruise the serpent's head is symbolic of all of the kingdom of darkness being under the feet of Christ. The head is often symbolic of the highest authority, much like how Jesus is the Head of His church (Colossians 1:18). So, when this verse says that Jesus will bruise the head of the kingdom of darkness, we know that it is referring to Jesus bruising the head of the highest ranked in the kingdom of darkness, satan himself. The highest in command in the kingdom of darkness has no control, and is being pinned down by the King of kings.

The fact that Jesus is on top, and satan is on the bottom is a symbolic parable showing that the realm where the enemy lives (the second heaven) is beneath where Christ reigns (the third heaven).

In Matthew 28:18 Jesus said, "All authority

has been given to Me in heaven and on earth." The word 'all' is a powerful word here. If Jesus has all authority, then guess who has no authority? Satan has no authority at all. Even though he has no authority, he does have power. Power and authority are two different things. A gun is a good symbol for power in the sense that it is dangerous and powerful. Whereas a policeman's badge is a good example of authority, in the sense that the one who carries the badge (authority) is the one in control and can stop a hectic situation with a single spoken word. The enemy may have some power and be able to shoot, but Jesus can stop him with a single word because He walks in something greater than only power. He wields both power and authority. This is why in Genesis 3:15, the serpent could still lash out to bruise a heel, because he has power, but he is not the one in control.

When we submit to a lie in assuming that the enemy indeed does have authority in our lives and circumstances, then we crown him with power. The reason why we crown him with with power, is because what we focus on we empower. When we give needless attention to something, our perception is that it is much bigger than it actually is. In Genesis, satan was condemned to slither on the ground as a serpent for the rest of eternity, yet in the book of Revelation he is described as a multi-headed dragon. Look at what we have turned him into by assuming that he has authority that does not actually belong to him. This is why it is important for us to understand our authority in our identity.

Romans 8:16-17: "The Spirit Himself bears witness with our spirit that we are children of God and if children, then heirs—heirs of God and joint heirs with Christ, if indeed we suffer with Him, that we may also be glorified together."

Do you know what it means to be a joint heir with Christ? It means that the very authority that was given to Jesus by the Father is also given to us. Not only is satan under Jesus' feet, but he is also under our feet. We know that in scripture Jesus was referred to as the last Adam (1 Corinthians 15:45) because He completed the mandate that Adam could not. Adam's mandate was to partake from the tree of life instead of from the knowledge of good and evil. This of course would result in Adam being fruitful and multiplying the culture of the garden of Eden, which was a place where heaven and Earth dwelled together, to be established to the ends of the earth. Where Adam failed, Jesus took up the baton to masterfully completed his mandate.

I believe there is a revelation being released on the earth where we are to understand that Adam was not called to walk out the mandate of being fruitful and multiplying to the ends of the earth alone. He was called to reign in the earth alongside his bride, Eve. Eve was called to walk as a co-heir with him. She was called to wield authority together with Adam. Genesis 3:20 says that Eve was destined to be the 'mother of all living'. She was a natural born queen. Since Eve failed to complete this mandate with her husband, Adam, just as God raised up a last Adam, He is also raising up the last Eve in these days to complete the 'first Eve's' mandate. The last Eve is the Bride of Christ who will reign alongside her husband Jesus, to marry the kingdom of heaven to the ends of the earth, making it the dwelling place for the glory of God.

You have a significant part to play in what is happening in the heavens. Jesus, the last Adam, is waiting for His Bride, the church, to stand up in her God-given authority. She is not a bruised and defeated Bride. She is the pure and spotless Bride who is victoriously triumphant through her Husband, Jesus Christ.

The kingdom of heaven is inside of you, which trumps the kingdom of darkness 100% of the time. It is in this place of revelation where we begin to see the enemy's attacks as more of an annoyance than as a threat.

Remember in Acts 16:16-18, when Paul the apostle was being followed by the girl who was demonized by a spirit of divination, and would tell fortunes? She followed him for days shouting about him. It says in verse 18 that Paul became greatly annoyed, so therefore cast the demon out of her. It did not say that he was concerned, or that she was a threat. He was simply annoyed by her outbursts. This speaks volumes to me about Paul's understanding of authority. He knew that the power that the demonic wielded did not even slightly compare to the power and authority that he held in Christ.

I say that to say this: the tactics of the enemy are under your feet. They should not scare you. You should not feel threatened by them. Through Christ we can have complete confidence in our royal identity in Him.

If you want to step out of fear of the demonic realm to stand in your full authority in Christ, then pray the following with me:

"Father God, Jesus, Holy Spirit, I repent from walking in a mindset of fear. I make the decision to believe that all authority has been given to You, Jesus. I make the decision to believe what the Word of God says that I am a co-heir with You. The same Spirit that raised You from the dead, is the same Spirit that dwells in me. Greater is He who is in me than he who is in the world. I make the decision now to stand in faith in the authority that I wield as a child of God, and as an ambassador of heaven."

Expelling the Darkness

Identity Breeds Authority

We have looked at how we carry authority in the heavenly realms. Now I want to discuss ways that we can influence the spirit realm. Even though this is not a book on deliverance ministry, because I am teaching on spiritual warfare, I feel it would be wise to cover some basics on this topic.

When Jesus walked the earth throughout the gospels, there were many manifestations seen throughout His ministry which were also seen in the Old Testament. Needless to say, Jesus did these things bigger and better than His predecessors. Jesus walked in healing and resurrection power just like Elijah and Elisha. Profound teachings were seen through Jesus' ministry, just as Ezra and the Levites taught the Israelites about the law (Nehemiah 8:6-8). Jesus came to shepherd a nation, just as Moses had. Yet, there was one manifestation in His public ministry that made Him distinctly different than the men and women of God who went before Him. This difference was that Jesus had an authority in the spirit realm which enabled Him to command demons to flee. There is no record of demons fleeing upon someones command in the Old Testament. The closest thing that I can find was when David would play his harp before King Saul and it would bring him deliverance from his torment (1 Samuel 16:23). However, as far as demons fleeing upon someone's command, Jesus was the first.

Mark 1:27: "Then they were all amazed, so that they questioned among themselves, saying, 'What is this? What new doctrine is this? For with authority He commands even the unclean spirits, and they obey Him.'"

The Bible is filled with stories of Jesus delivering people from demonic spirits. I will list scriptures for you to look up on your own time to build your faith:

Matthew 4:10-11	Luke 13:32
Luke 11:14	Luke 4:33-36
Matthew 8:16	Matthew 8:28-32
Mark 1:32-34	Mark 5:1-13
Luke 4:40-41	Luke 8:26-39
Mark 1:39	Mark 9:25-27
Matthew 9:32-33	Mark 16:9

Not only did Jesus see many delivered by His word, but He trained and equipped others to do the same. In Matthew 10:8 Jesus commissioned His disciples saying, "Heal the sick, cleanse the lepers, raise the dead, cast out demons. Freely you have received, freely give."

Jesus had a constant awareness of not only the spirit realm, but also of the spiritual battle occurring around Him. Throughout Jesus' ministry He was fulfilling the prophecy spoken in Genesis 3:15 to wage warfare against the kingdom of darkness.

Jesus knew who the Father said He was, and this is what permitted Him to walk in excellence concerning His deliverance ministry. Receiving the blessing of the Father is what sets us apart to walk in authority, as opposed to operating out of insecurity. Authority has everything to do with understanding your identity. Knowing your identity has everything to do with being rooted in the secret place with God, to reform your mind in what the Father says about you. Jesus made intimacy and relationship with His Father His first priority (John 5:19-20). I believe that this is the difference between the deliverance ministry of Jesus compared to the attempt at deliverance of the sons of Sceva in Acts 19:13-16.

Acts 19:13-16: "Then some of the itinerant Jewish exorcists took it upon themselves to call the name of the Lord Jesus over those who had evil spirits, saying, 'We exorcise you by the Jesus whom Paul preaches.' Also there were seven sons of Sceva, a Jewish chief priest, who did so. And the evil spirit answered and said, 'Jesus I know, and Paul I know; but who are you?' Then the man in whom the evil spirit was leaped on them, overpowered them, and prevailed against them, so that they fled out of that house naked and wounded."

The sons of Sceva were not able to walk in full authority and were abused by this demon because they did not understand who they were in Christ. They did not know who they were to such an extent that the demon did not even recognize who they were.

When God was commissioning Moses in Exodus 3 to help deliver the Israelites, Moses asked God who he should say sent him. God responded saying "'I Am who I Am.' And He said, 'Thus you shall say to the children of Israel, 'I AM has sent me to you.'" Jesus is the great I AM because He is completely confident in who He is, not willing to compromise Himself. He is not in an identity crisis, and therefore does not need to impress anyone to appease insecurities. When we do not know who we are, yet try to move in this form of authority, it is not true authority. It is instead insecurity masquerading as authority. This is what separated Jesus from the sons of Sceva. Jesus knew who He was, where the sons of Sceva did not. It is when we are trying to move in authority out of insecurity when we start getting ourselves into trouble concerning deliverance ministry.

I have heard different people involved in deliverance ministry share stories about the more intense deliverances that they have experienced while ministering. They would share about how these extended deliverances were filled with times where the demon would manifest through people in such a way that the people performing the deliverance would be physically harmed. They would share this as though to say, "sometimes the demons are just that strong." Although I do know that there are times for extended deliverances, we should never be in a mentality that the demons are "just that strong". I am not opposed to vulnerably sharing stories that went wrong because we were learning and growing in our authority. However, we should never magnify the demonic as though to say that this is how deliverance should be at times, simply because we are not walking in a greater revelation of authority as of yet.

Bringing heaven to earth through authority has everything to do with knowing who you are in God's kingdom. Jesus said that the kingdom of heaven is within us (Luke 17:21), showing that we are actually carriers of the perfect culture of heaven. You are a powerful person. I have often shared this story, even in other writings because I feel that it is a good example of kingdom authority.

I remember a time when I was visiting a church that was being pastored by a friend of mine. I was walking throughout the building checking the place out, when I saw a group of people yelling and screaming. I looked closer and saw that the group was gathered around a woman who was laying on a mat. One of the women who recognized me ran over to me and started explaining the situation. She told me that the woman who was being prayed over had been a paralytic for nine years and that she had to bring a mat with her everywhere she went. The woman continued to tell me that the group had been praying over her for an extended amount of time, and they had not seen any breakthrough.

I walked over to the woman on the mat and saw that she was frantic because of everyone yelling, screaming and rebuking demons around her. I was able to discern that her pain was, in fact, rooted in a demonic stronghold. However, these people were going about it in the wrong way. There are times to shout, but if you feel that the demonic will only move if you raise your voice, then you are putting more trust in your natural tone than in your spiritual authority. You carry such authority that even the faintest whisper from you can make the mightiest demons flee. I told everyone who was there to stop shouting and praying, because it was making this woman frantic. I sat down on the ground with the woman, took her hand and whispered to her, "You know, this can be a lot easier than all of these people are making it out to be." I helped her up off her mat and her body completely straightened out. The demonic stronghold was immediately broken. She was healed and set free in an instant.

Wisdom Concerning Deliverance Ministry

So how is it that deliverance was such a staple in the ministry of Jesus, yet in church culture we often do not hear of it? I believe that one of the reasons many have rejected the legitimacy of deliverance ministry is because it has been abused in the past. It makes sense that the enemy would try to taint the reputation of something that was such a prominent part of the ministry of Jesus.

There was a time in the church where there was a restoration of our mandate concerning deliverance ministry. Many in the church began to understand their authority in Christ over unclean spirits, much like the disciples began to understand in Matthew 10:8 during the great commission. Often when God releases a new revelation to the church, as we are learning to grow into maturity, there are some who bring that revelation to an unhealthy extreme. This usually occurs due to a lack of experience and discernment. This is what happened when a revelation of authority was released over the church. When this happened with the present church, many began to have such a focus on the manifestation of the demonic that they forgot about the people who were being delivered.

Instead of deliverance ministry being about seeing people set free from torment, for many it became a curiosity concerning the supernatural. For others it went a step further where they would pray for people to manifest a demon, then would begin to draw attention to what was happening so they would be deemed as "spiritually mature" in the eyes of men. This is often what can happen when we begin to move in power but do not allow Jesus to take leadership over what is happening. We begin to minister out of insecurity and pride instead of a genuine love for people. However, even though there have been abuses in the area of deliverance ministry, wisdom says not to throw away the blessing with the curse. We need to, instead, learn from our mistakes so that we can see this ministry mature from a place of adolescence into adulthood.

For the sake of giving you an idea of what unhealthy deliverance ministry could look like, I will share a story with you:

One time, I was ministering overseas at a conference where I was one of many speakers. For the most part the conference was very good, until one of the speakers began to minister at the end of one of the evenings. Now, I want to clarify something. I am not saying this to shame this speaker. It is never my heart to dishonour anyone, which is why I am not sharing this particular person's name. However, this person was demonstrating a dysfunctional side of deliverance ministry, which many have slipped into. I believe that it is something that needs to be addressed for the sake of people being honoured.

This minister would stand in the front and call someone up before everyone; most often, a teenager. The speaker would then look into the person's eyes until they would begin weeping hysterically and dramatically manifesting a demon. The person would then travail and shake on the ground, shrieking. The speaker would not even cast the demon out, but would leave that person to call up another. Pastors would then come around the person on the ground and would begin shouting over them in an attempt to cast out the demon. People would gather around watching, as though it were a show.

My jaw dropped as I watched this happen. This speaker seemed to forget that these were people this was happening to. It is one thing to cast out a demon, but when that demon is being forced to leave someone, as a last mandate, it tries to humiliate the person it is leaving. This is exactly what was taking place. These people were being delivered in a very poor and dishonouring way, and were being put on display in front of their family and friends. They were being demonized, and branded as a person who once writhed on the floor chaotically.

Once there were about three teenagers convulsing on the ground, I'd had about enough. People were not taking into consideration that these people were being publicly tormented. I started walking up to the teenagers who were on the ground, would squeeze between the pastors who were shouting out deliverance prayers and would lay a single finger on the person. Since the music was blaring and the pastors were shouting, they would not have been able to hear me. All that I said in a faint whisper was, "Shut up, and get out."

Immediately, the person on the floor would stop shrieking and convulsing, would stand up and go sit down. I did this person after person to save the dignity of those who were being delivered.

When a spirit from the second heaven (the

spirit realm) manifests in the natural realm, we have the right to deal with it accordingly. However, we need to take the people who are being delivered into consideration. Our heart posture cannot be to move in deliverance simply out of a curiosity of the supernatural. Nor should we have a heart posture to want to see a manifestation simply because we are insecure and want to look spiritual. We need to do it because we love the person and want them to be set free. When we come under the direction of Jesus as our leader, loving people with honour becomes the priority and we are guided by wisdom. Jesus never used people to make a scene in His ministry. You may have noticed in the verses that I listed earlier that He kept deliverances quick and to the point. He did this because He understood that a demon fleeing was not about Him or making His ministry look good. It was about the person experiencing freedom.

From experience, I know that often a sign of someone being delivered from a demon is that they begin to dry heave or throw up. However, there are many Spirit led groups in the world that are beginning to understand that throwing up is not a pleasant thing to experience while being set free. It would also not be pleasant for the person who would need to clean it up. So, when a demon would begin to manifest in this way, forcing someone to throw up, they instead command the demon to stop manifesting that way and to come out quietly. This all comes back to honouring people. Someone experiencing deliverance should not have to deal with emotional trauma and fear from being set free.

Luke 10:17-20: "Then the seventy returned with joy, saying, 'Lord, even the demons are subject to us in Your name.' And He said to them, 'I saw Satan fall like lightning from heaven. Behold, I give you the authority to trample on serpents and scorpions, and over all the power of the enemy, and nothing shall by any means hurt you. Nevertheless do not rejoice in this, that the spirits are subject to you, but rather rejoice because your names are written in heaven.'"

When the disciples came back after the great commission, they were overzealous about the authority they had over the demonic. Jesus acknowledged what they said, but then instantly told them that this was not something they should rejoice in and pointed them back to salvation. See, there was something about the disciples' over-emphasis on spiritual manifestation that made Jesus uncomfortable. He had to correct them, knowing that if their focus remained on only the manifestations that their attentions would have been taken off of people and their salvation. This could have eventually stopped the sweeping revival that was taking place; whereas if they kept their eyes on the salvation of Christ, they would eventually see the nations transformed through their ministry.

A pivotal principal that we should know concerning deliverance ministry is found in Matthew 12:43-45. Jesus was speaking and said, "When an unclean spirit goes out of a man, he goes through dry places, seeking rest, and finds none. Then he says, 'I will return to my house from which I came.' And when he comes, he finds it empty, swept, and put in order. Then he goes and takes with him seven other spirits more wicked than himself, and they enter and dwell there; and the last state of that man is worse than the first. So shall it also be with this wicked generation."

I have seen many wild deliverances in the church and also on the streets, while ministering to people who do not yet know Jesus. However, if I am ministering to someone in the marketplace who does not yet know Jesus, I need to keep this principle in mind if I am moving in a direction of deliverance. I believe that this is one of the reasons why Jesus directed the disciples back to salvation when they were so zealous about demons fleeing in Luke 10:17-20. Jesus knew that if the disciples only focused on seeing deliverances and were not focused on the fullness of salvation, that the people being delivered would not receive the Spirit of God through salvation to fill the void that was left by the demonic.

One of my mentors mentioned to me that he needs to be discerning when people come to him in meetings asking him to pray for deliverance for them. He said that sometimes witches in the occult would come to his meetings asking for deliverance prayers, but would not receive Holy Spirit after being delivered. They did this purposely because they understood the spiritual principal that if they did not receive Holy Spirit, then they would actually become more powerful in the occult. This is because the demon that fled them would rally more demons to fill the void that was left.

There have been times while ministering outside of the church where I would see someone saved, then would be led by the Spirit of God to see them delivered. There are also times when I would see someone delivered and then this would open the door for them to commit to Christ. However, I would not move in deliverance with someone who would not be willing to receive Jesus in the area of their lives where they have been delivered. When we receive Christ, we receive the Spirit of God. I would not want to cast out a demon if that person were not willing to receive Christ, because the Spirit of God would not be filling the void where the demon or demons have left. This would likely leave the person in a worse state than before since that demon would go to grab seven of its friends worse than itself, to inhabit the person again.

Some of you might be asking yourself, "Is it not when we are baptized in the Spirit, like in Acts 2, when we are filled with Holy Spirit?" The Spirit of God fills us when we receive Christ as our Lord and Saviour. When we are baptized in the Holy

Spirit, the Spirit of God comes upon us. There is a distinct difference. Remember the disciples in John 20:22? This occurred after Jesus had died on the cross for mankind. He breathed upon His disciples to receive Holy Spirit internally, for their sakes. Acts 2 is when the Spirit of God came upon the disciples for the sake of others. This was to allow others to experience Holy Spirit through them. Acts 2 was what Jesus experienced when Holy Spirit came upon Him like a dove in Luke 3:22, when He was commissioned into ministry on the earth. Jesus was already filled with Holy Spirit before this, but Holy Spirit came upon Him to baptize Him in the form of a dove.

So, when we are moving in deliverance, wisdom tells us that this person should have the Spirit of God abiding in them, or will need to receive Jesus in the area of their lives that they were delivered. Otherwise we risk seeing them freed in an area, but not receive Holy Spirit to fill the void.

Discerning of Spirits

1 Corinthians 12:7-10: "The manifestation of the Spirit is given to each one for the profit of all: for to one is given the word of wisdom through the Spirit, to another the word of knowledge through the same Spirit, to another faith by the same Spirit, to another gifts of healings by the same

Spirit, to another the working of miracles, to another prophecy, to another discerning of spirits, to another different kinds of tongues, to another the interpretation of tongues."

The gift of discerning of spirits is an excellent tool to pair with deliverance ministry. Since I have already done extensive work in writing on discernment gifts, I will keep this brief and strictly pertaining to deliverance ministry.

One place where we go wrong in discerning of spirits is that those who walk in this gift often limit themselves with only walking in a fraction of the gift. I believe that the gift of discerning of spirits is one of the most misunderstood gifts recorded in 1 Corinthians 12. It is misunderstood because people have often limited this gift to just discerning demonic spirits. One of the purposes for discerning of spirits is to discern demonic spirits; however, this is probably only 20% of the gift's function.

Discerning of spirits is not specifically called 'discerning of demonic spirits'. Rather, it is more general than specific. This gift is also for discerning angelic spirits, human spirits, and most importantly, to discern what Holy Spirit is doing.

Contrary to popular belief, the key to seeing people set free has less to do with discerning demons, than it has to do with discerning what

Holy Spirit is saying. When we are only discerning what is happening with the demonic and are not discerning what Holy Spirit wants to do in a situation, we may know how the person is being tormented, but we will not know the road to lead them to freedom. When we do not discern what Holy Spirit is saying, we begin to depend on our own human logic. This allows for the potential to step into an unhealthy dependancy on systems for deliverance ministry.

How Holy Spirit leads you to see someone delivered one time, may not be the same as the next time. I have seen many people delivered from different spirits, yet the deliverances have been quite diverse. There have been times when I would simply speak to a spirit and command it to leave. Other times Holy Spirit would have me lead them through a time of forgiveness. Still, other times where the Lord would show me the root where the enemy had a foothold in their heart.

I have seen many deliverance ministries operate based on certain systems to see people set free. There are certainly Biblical truths which we can apply as a map for freedom, such as how forgiveness is a pivotal key for healing. There are also specific strategies that God will give in the form of systems to bring people to healing. However, if we are following a system over and above the Spirit of God, then we are believing that God will do the exact same thing every time in every situation. This would be to believe that God is more mechanical than organic, which would contradict His nature. If we want to be used to a greater extent in seeing people set free, we need to learn to discern what Holy Spirit is saying. When we can learn to discern His voice, we will be able to receive the different keys for people's healing.

Discerning of spirits has two steps to it. First, we discern what is occurring externally. Second, we discern internally what the Spirit of God is saying about it. I know many who move in this type of gifting, yet feel burdened when they discern something. They do not know how to discern the voice of God to know what to do about what they are perceiving. They feel as though they have spiritual insight and information, yet do not know the practical application. Logically trying to figure out how to deal with what you discern could get you in a lot of trouble. It could even lead you down a path of believing that everything you discern is your responsibility to deal with. If that were the case, spiritually discerning people would burn out very quickly. Sometimes you discern things because Holy Spirit wants to give insight into how to bring change. Other times, we discern things simply because we are discerning. Our responsibility is to be in communication with Holy Spirit and to keep in step with what He is doing and saying.

If you want to grow to greater levels of maturity in deliverance ministry and discernment, I want you to pray this with me:

"Holy Spirit, I pray for a deeper revelation of the authority that You have given me. I repent for any time that I may not have viewed deliverance ministry in a healthy light. I repent for any times that I may have operated in deliverance ministry out of an unhealthy mindset. I pray that You would give me a deep love for people. Give me Your heart for others, Father. Use me as a vessel to bring healing and change to those who are oppressed and tormented. Teach me to be a vessel to bring freedom. I pray for an increase in my ability to hear Your voice. I pray for an increase in the gift of discerning of spirits, for the sake of seeking Your children experience freedom."

Kingdom Intercession

We often view prayer through the lens of fighting towards victory, instead of from the perspective that we already reign in a place of victory. Prayer is a powerful tool that we have the privilege of wielding in order to help forcefully advance the kingdom of God. The word intercession translated from the Hebrew means, 'to meet'. Intercession is just that. It is meeting with God in prayer on behalf of someone or something.

One thing I have learned about intercession is that when we pray, we are not praying to change God's mind. Look at this:

2 Chronicles 7:14: "If My people who are called by My name will humble themselves, and pray and seek My face, and turn from their wicked ways, then I will hear from heaven, and will forgive their sin and heal their land."

When God says something like this, He is not asking us to pray for the purpose of convincing Him to heal our land. God's heart is already to bring healing to communities, cities and nations. However, since the beginning, it has always been God's heart to co-labour with mankind to bridge the kingdom of heaven to Earth. This is what prayer and intercession is. It is an opportunity to discern the heart and will of God and to agree in prayer and declaration to bring it into existence.

Romans 8:34: "Who is he who condemns? It is Christ who died, and furthermore is also risen, who is even at the right hand of God, who also makes intercession for us."

True strategic intercession is discerning what Jesus is already interceding for. It is discerning what is on His heart, and partnering with Him in prayer. This requires having ears that are attuned to the word of the Lord. When the leading of Holy Spirit can be bound to our intercession, then our prayers and declarations will become less like loose cannons, and instead more precise and strategic.

We can see in scripture that our prayers have a direct impact on what is occurring in the spirit realm. I truly believe that many of the breakthroughs I have seen in my life and ministry are as a result of the prayers of others. I have assigned intercessors who cover my ministry in prayer because I know that their prayers are pivotal to the impact that we see throughout the nations.

Mark 9 shares a story about when the disciples had tried to cast a demon out of a man's son, yet could not. The boy was brought to Jesus in Mark 9:25 and Jesus said, "Deaf and dumb spirit, I command you, come out of him and enter him no more!" The demon fled the boy, and the disciples asked Jesus why they could not cast out the spirit. Jesus responded in verse 29 saying, "This kind can come out by nothing but prayer and fasting."

Jesus shows us something remarkable in this verse. The first thing He shows us is that, when He walked the earth, He understood principals about prayer and fasting that we still do not fully comprehend. This is why if we want to make an eternal imprint through our prayers, it would be wise to partner with our great Intercessor instead of praying on our own. Secondly, He shows us that what we pray in the natural realm shifts things drastically in the spirit realm. Looking at this verse, I believe that it is safe to assume that Jesus had cultivated a lifestyle of prayer and fasting, which gave Him full authority to cast out the demon. It was what He was doing in the natural that shifted the spiritual.

Often, while waiting for a breakthrough, what we do not realize is that our lack of willingness to co-labour with Jesus in intercession and declaration could be what is postponing our breakthrough.

Several years ago, the Lord began to speak to me concerning a revival which was going to take place in a particular city. He told me that this city had been pregnant with revival for many years and that for the next two years the city would be in labour to give birth to a move of God. Holy Spirit showed me that the contractions from the labour will be the intercession of the church calling out to God to see heaven dwelling on Earth. I, together with a group of people who God had highlighted very clearly, committed to two years of very intentional intercession.

At least one evening a week, and sometimes two or three times per week, we would spend the night praying for revival to break loose in that city. We would all listen to Holy Spirit and would pray and declare God's prophetic word in intercession. We made an intentional point in trying our best to discern the heart of Jesus for this city, and would partner with Him. For two years straight we lifted up different churches and pastors in prayer. There were times when God would have us even study to learn about the history of the city for prayer purposes. We learned much about the city's spiritual climate. We knew what communities were key to the city for citywide breakthrough.

After two years of praying and interceding, we saw a great outpouring in the city. The birthing of revival took place. Churches and pastors began to be united. People were beginning to not stumble over denominational barriers. We saw many salvations and countless miracles, signs and wonders.

Now, it would be very easy to look at something like this and assume that the reconciliation between pastors, salvations, miracles, signs and wonders would have taken place whether or not we set aside that time to pray. We assume things such as this because we do not perceive what is taking place in the spirit realm. I, personally, do not think that revival would have been birthed in such a way if we, and others like us, were not praying. I believe that God was looking for people who would discern that His heart was for revival in this city, and would be willing to intercede with Him.

There were many times throughout this two year season where God showed me what was taking place in the heavenly realms through our prayers. There is no doubt in my mind that our prayers not only influenced what was occurring in the spirit realm, but was greatly instrumental to the revival that was birthed in this city.

Intercession Pitfalls

I want to bring some clarity concerning two common prophetic intercession pitfalls.

The first pitfall I want to address is a mindset of 'ground warfare'. I have met many intercessors who carry a sphere of heaviness and sometimes depression. Often intercessors will feel the burden of people and of the Lord, which gives them instruction in how to pray. However if the burden feels heavy and does not lift after the intercession is finished, then something is off. We need to understand that God's yoke is easy and His burden is light (Matthew 11:30).

The reason why intercessors can fall into this pitfall is because of a misunderstanding of where they are seated. Intercessors will often have gifts of discerning of spirits, so they will often discern what is happening in the demonic realm. This gives them clarity on how to pray. While this discernment can be helpful, it can also cause issues if the intercessor takes a posture in prayer that attempts to war against the demonic realm. We discussed earlier that we are not seated where the demonic realm is. We need to understand this, especially when we are posturing ourselves in prayer and intercession. Our job is not to battle demons in the second heaven. Our job is to walk in the revelation that we are seated in heavenly placcs in Christ (Ephesians 2:6). Intercession does not have anything to do with "fighting the demonic". It has everything to do with seeing things from heaven's perspective and from the place of intimacy with God. From that place we can declare life. This disqualifies any form of ground warfare and invites us into properly co-reigning with Christ.

As we learn to pray that which is on the heart of God, we will begin to understand that our job in intercession is not to take on prayer mandates that simply accommodate to the need. We need to be able to discern those mandates that are actually ours to be praying into. I have met different intercessors who have taken it upon themsclves to try to dethrone demonic principalities over cities or nations. They have ended up in extreme demonic torment and bondage because they have overstepped their boundaries in what the Lord has asked them to take on. While I would not go as far as to say that there are never strategic times to pray into such things, we should not be toying with things as serious as this. We need to be content in knowing that some battles are the Lord's, and should not try to run ahead of our General in spiritual warfare. We need to trust Him to lead us.

Even the archangel Michael understood not to take on battles that were not mandated of the Lord. We can see this in Jude 1:9: "Yet Michael the archangel, in contending with the devil, when he disputed about the body of Moses, dared not bring against him a reviling accusation, but said, 'The Lord rebuke you!'"

We are all a part of God's army, and we need to learn to partner with our General, Jesus, in intercession. We are not to be beneath Him, where the angels and demons battle. Nor are we supposed to be running ahead of Him, taking our own lead. We need to trust His lead, co-labouring with Him to bridge heaven to Earth.

The second pitfall I want to address concerning intercession is 'improper decrees'. People who are more seasoned and refined in intercession do not often struggle with this, but it can be an issue for those who are just beginning to walk in their authority in prayer and declaration.

An elementary principal concerning intercession is understanding that your words have power. Look at these verses:

Proverbs 18:21: "Death and life are in the power of the tongue, And those who love it will eat its fruit."

Job 22:28: "You will also declare a thing, And it will be established for you; So light will shine on your ways."

All of creation was brought into existence through prophetic declaration. God did not think, 'let there be light' and there was light. He spoke it and light manifested. Since we are kings and queens who were created in the direct image of the all-powerful God, our declarations carry tremendous weight.

I once heard a man who was very high up in a well-established ministry teach on this subject. He shared a story of a male staff member who worked for him who was going through a rough time emotionally, yet had no clue why he was struggling. This man was in his early thirties and was not married. After asking the Lord why he was feeling so bogged down emotionally, the Lord began to reveal to him that there had been various women who were praying to God and declaring that they would one day marry him. They obviously prayed this because of his placement and success in ministry. This man then gathered a few friends to pray over him to break these words off of him, and he was instantly set free from his emotional turmoil.

Often, undeveloped or new intercessors can slip into viewing circumstances through their own desires instead of God's desires. Therefore, they will begin declaring what they want instead of declaring God's will. I am of course talking more about declarations concerning direction for others. When things are Biblically God's will, such as healing, freedom and salvation for others, you can declare away. However, when it comes to the free will and direction of people, then it is best not to move into declaration as you could be uncertain of God's will for that person.

An example would be if a relative of yours wanted to quit their job to move to a new job. You might be uncertain if this is God's will for them or not, so saying things like, "I declare that they will stay at their current job", might actually be warring against what God truly wants for them. Remember, your words have power and if you are simply praying for and declaring what you want instead of what God wants, you could be warring against the will of God for someone's life. This structure of declarative prayer can be a form of Christian witchcraft. Any form of manipulation is witchcraft because it takes away free will through control.

Knowing the authority that our words have, we need to be a people who will dedicate our tongues to God to only speak life and truth.

The soul makes a terrible leader. We cannot be lead by our emotions. Our soul needs to come under submission to the Spirit of God while we are stepping into prayer and intercession.

Fasting

In Mark 9:29, when Jesus said to His disciples, "This kind (demon) can come out by nothing but prayer and fasting", we can see that it was not only prayer that brought breakthrough in the spirit realm. Jesus revealed that fasting is a profound tool to shift what is occurring in the heavens as well. I believe that fasting is an often forgotten, yet powerful tool for intercession.

Some believe that fasting is only for some; however, if we understood the benefits of fasting, I think we would think differently. In Matthew 6:17-18, Jesus teaches on fasting, saying, "When you fast, anoint your head and wash your face, so that you do not appear to men to be fasting, but to your Father who is in the secret place; and your Father who sees in secret will reward you openly." Notice how this verse does not start out saying, "If you fast." It says, "when you fast," implying that you will.

Fasting in intercession can do powerful things in the spirit realm. As I mentioned in the introduction, it was through fasting that this book was birthed.

We can see a powerful example of the power of fasting in Daniel 10. After a vision that Daniel had, he began a fast which lasted three weeks. Daniel said in Daniel 10:3, "I ate no pleasant food, no meat or wine came into my mouth, nor did I anoint myself at all, till three whole weeks were fulfilled."

Once Daniel's fast was complete, Daniel fell into a vision where an angel came to him. The angel said to Daniel in Daniel 10:12-13, "Do not fear, Daniel, for from the first day that you set your heart to understand, and to humble yourself before your God, your words were heard; and I have come because of your words. But, the prince of the kingdom of Persia withstood me twenty-one days; and behold, Michael, one of the chief princes, came to help me, for I had been left alone there with the kings of Persia."

This is profound to me. Daniel fasted for exactly 21 days, and this angel tells Daniel that it had been withstood from a demonic force for exactly 21 days. It seems as though Daniel's fasting and prayer enabled the angel Michael to free the angel in order to speak with Daniel. Daniel's fasting directly influenced what was occurring in the spirit realm.

When we are simply listening to the Spirit of God and obeying, we have no clue what is being accomplished in the unseen realm. You have no idea what breakthroughs are taking place in the heavenly realms simply because of your intercession and fasting.

Partnering with Angels

As prophetic people, we need to understand that when we prophesy, we are actually partnering with the angelic by commissioning them into their God given mandate. This ties strongly into prophetic intercession.

Ephesians 3:8-10: "To me, who am less than the least of all the saints, this grace was given, that I should preach among the Gentiles the unsearchable riches of Christ, and to make all see what is the fellowship of the mystery, which from the beginning of the ages has been hidden in God who created all things through Jesus Christ; to the intent that now the manifold wisdom of God might be made known by the church to the principalities and powers in the heavenly places."

This verse says that the wisdom of God is made known to the principalities and powers in the heavenly realms through His church. When Paul refers to principalities and powers, he is referring to different angelic ranks. If you look at Ephesians 6:12, it talks about the different demonic rankings. It says, "For we do not wrestle against flesh and blood, but against principalities, against powers, against the rulers of the darkness of this age, against spiritual hosts of wickedness in the heavenly places."

The book of Daniel gives us three examples of different celestial principalities. Let's look at Daniel 10 again since it holds so many profound truths concerning the spirit realm. An angel was speaking to the prophet Daniel in Daniel 10:13 saying, "But the prince of the kingdom of Persia withstood me twenty-one days; and behold, Michael, one of the chief princes, came to help me, for I had been left alone there with the kings of Persia."

Daniel 10:20-21: "Then he said, 'Do you know why I have come to you? And now I must return to fight with the prince of Persia; and when I have gone forth, indeed the prince of Greece will come. But I will tell you what is noted in the Scripture of Truth. (No one upholds me against these, except Michael your prince.)'"

Daniel 10 mentions two demonic principalities (the prince of Persia and the prince of Greece), and mentions one angelic principality (Michael). Ephesians 3:10 says that the church will make the wisdom of God known to the principalities and powers in heavenly places. This implies that since we have Holy Spirit abiding in us, we actually have a deeper revelation of the strategy of the Lord than the angels do. 1 Peter 1:12 says, "To them (the Old Testament prophets) it was revealed that, not to themselves, but to us they were ministering the things which now have been reported to you through those who have preached the gospel to you by the Holy Spirit sent from heaven - things which angels desire to look into."

Through the prophetic ministry, prophetic intercession and by declaring the word of the Lord, we are releasing the wisdom and strategy of the Lord to angels, and assigning them mandates. Look at Revelation 2 and 3. When John writes to the churches, he did not write the word of the Lord to the pastor, apostle or leader of Ephesus or Sardis. It says, "To the angel of the church of Ephesus write: ..." John's word from the Lord actually commissioned angels into their mandates. As the church continues to practice prophetic declaration and intercession, we can expect to see the kingdom advancing since we are partnering alongside of heavenly hosts in the heavenly realms.

Let's take some time to pray to close off the chapter:

"Jesus, my General, teach me to intercede with You. Help me to not fall behind You. Help me to not run ahead of You. Help me to be with You. Show me what is on Your heart. Teach me to pray with You. Help me to cultivate a lifestyle of fasting and prayer. Let my intercession advance Your kingdom. Let it empower the angels in the spirit

realm, that Your will would be accomplished on Earth as it is in heaven."

External Warfare

In medieval time periods, men were stationed upon city walls to watch for the enemy. They would stand watch to discern the enemy's strategy. God wants to raise us up as watchmen and watchwomen on the wall, that we may understand the enemy's strategy and how to stand in authority, while at the same time, resting in Christ. Throughout the next few chapters I will be focusing on the enemy's strategy in warfare towards us. I want to preface this by saying that our focus should never be towards the demonic. Nor is it my heart to bring an unhealthy focus in writing so deliberately on this topic. However, it would be foolish not to allow ourselves to be equipped in learning how to counter his schemes.

There are three types of warfare I am going to discuss throughout this book. The first one I will cover is External Warfare. Secondly, I will teach on

Practical Warfare. Lastly, you will read about Internal Warfare. Obviously, these specific terms are not found in scripture. However, they are headings I am using to better explain Biblical examples I have found in scripture and have experienced personally.

External warfare occurs when the enemy tries to invade your life from the outside in. He tries to sway you in this manner when he does not have a foothold in your heart. An excellent example of this is found in Matthew 4 when Jesus was tempted by satan. The enemy had no place in the heart of Jesus, so therefore tried to sway Him externally from a place of sonship to orphanship. He was trying to sway Jesus from a place of faith to a place of doubt.

For us to fully understand this concept, we need to be able to comprehend the enemy's strategy in warfare. I have heard people try to intellectualize the concept of spiritual warfare, making it seem overly intricate. However, the enemy's tactic in spiritual warfare is incredibly simple. It is to make us lose sight of our identity so we forget to stand in our birthright as royal sons and daughters of God. He wants to shift our perspective of how we view ourselves, to move us from a place of faith to a place of fear.

The enemy knows that if you are not walking in the revelation that you are a son or daughter, you are immobilized from experiencing the fullness of God's blessing in your life. He wants to rob you of your joy and peace. Not only does he want to rob you of your birthright, but he does not want you to understand how powerful you truly are. He knows that if you are walking in the fullness of your identity in Christ, not only will you experience the blessings of God, but everyone you come into contact with will experience them as well, through you.

In Matthew 3:17, Jesus is baptized by John the Baptist. There was a voice that came down from heaven in that moment that said, "This is My beloved Son, in whom I am well pleased." In that moment Jesus received a blessing of sonship from His Father. His identity was reaffirmed.

Now, the very next chapter, Matthew 4, is the chapter where Jesus is tempted by satan in the wilderness for 40 days. You will notice that the very first thing that satan says to Him is, "If you really are the Son of God..." and would then go on with tempting Him. This is important for us to take note of. The first thing the enemy attacked, right after Jesus received His blessing from His Father concerning sonship, is His sonship. He attacked His identity. With external warfare, the enemy's first priority was to make Jesus lose sight of Himself, and try to make Him forget what His Father said about Him.

One of the interesting things about warfare is that it is much more common to experience than you might think. One of the enemy's main objectives throughout your day is to accomplish this very thing, to sway you from your true identity. It is to make you believe that you are an orphan instead of a son or daughter. It is to make you believe that you are a peasant instead of royalty.

Have you ever had an experience where you were going about your day, feeling completely fine, when all of a sudden you feel a sudden stab of anxiety or insecurity? You were doing fine, but all of a sudden you found yourself in a place of fear and a lack of confidence. This is a basic form of spiritual warfare. You were standing in a place of faith and confidence, when all of a sudden the enemy began planting thoughts in your head to strike fear and doubt.

I remember a time when my wife and I entered full time ministry. I was brought on as the assistant pastor at a church. It was a new church plant and did not have the finances to pay us for pastoring, so it was our responsibility to raise funds. These few years of pastoring, believing for finances by faith became a wild rollercoaster of ups and downs. It was a constant test of faith, where God was continually shaping in us hearts that knew He was our Provider. I wish I could say that I was always able to stand in full faith, knowing that God would provide, but I would be lying to you. There were absolutely times when I stood in faith, yet there were other times when I felt fear and doubt.

One month specifically, we were very short financially. I remember the feeling on the last day of the month when we had to pay rent the very next day, yet did not have a single dime to our name. To top it off, we had a church service that evening at which I was speaking. I remember trying to teach and minister, attempting to avoid looking at the clock because I was counting down the hours until I had to face my landlord with no rent. Unrealistic thoughts were flooding my mind about all of the terrible things that could happen to us because of this. One part of me was saying that I was a son of God and that my Father would provide on time. On the other hand, I was a ball of stress and anxiety, panicking in an attempt to think of what to do. There was a battle going on in my mind. One side was calling me son, the other was telling me that I was an orphan.

After I finished speaking, I remember sitting on one of the pews when I was notified that an anonymous person wanted to donate personally to my wife and I. When I asked how much money he had donated, it was the exact amount that we needed for rent the next day, to the penny.

Even though there was much that took place throughout those three years, in our whole time of pastoring, we were never once at lack. God provided every single time, and now we have a stack of supernatural financial testimonies from that time. That time of believing set our foundation of faith concerning finances for when we would step into ministry on a grander scale.

The battlefield for warfare is the mind. You can see in this story that the enemy was trying to sway me from my place of faith with seeds of doubt. The enemy will try to plant lies in your mind so that you will begin to put faith in those lies. When we empower the lies, it taints our perception of how we view ourselves. It taints our view of who God is. The enemy wants to hide truth with a web of lies.

In Daniel 1, the prophet Daniel and his three friends Hananiah, Mishael and Azariah were brought into king Nebuchadnezzar's service. While entering their training to serve the king, they were given new names. Daniel (which means God is my judge) was called Belteshazzar (meaning lord of the straitened's treasure). Hananiah was named Shadrach; to Mishael was given the name Meshach; and to Azariah, Abednego. This was actually a brainwashing technique. Nebuchadnezzar tried to take away their names which glorified God, to give them new names which instead glorified his own gods. He was trying to trick them into believing they were someone who they were not. He was trying to rewrite their identities. This is the enemy's tactic of warfare.

I have spoken with many people who have at times been going about their days, when all of a sudden, an image would come into their minds about them doing something that would be oddly out of character for them. These could be things such as drinking excessively, bursting out in anger or looking at something like pornography. This would leave them feeling confused because these are not things they would normally struggle with. Why would they experience this? It is because the enemy is trying to plant lies in their minds, hoping that they would manifest in their hearts, causing a person to veer off course from their true identity.

This is essentially what happened with Adam and Eve, through the serpent in Genesis 2. Adam and Eve did not originally have sin in their hearts. They walked in full intimacy and friendship with the Lord, experiencing His goodness continuously. Yet, satan approached them and began to wage war on their minds. He began feeding them lies. Adam and Eve then allowed those lies to infiltrate their hearts, resulting in external sin.

We need a revelation that grips us, so that we will know that we are truly powerful people in Christ. When we understand that we are powerful people, we are able to comprehend the fact that just because something is happening around you externally, does not mean that it needs to affect your internal culture. Just because something enters your mind, does not mean that it needs to enter your heart.

The financial story that I shared with you is a very tame story regarding spiritual warfare. Many of you reading this book I am sure have experienced more extreme levels of warfare. I will share with you a more intense story with the purpose of showing you that, even though there may be different extremes in warfare, the enemy's tactic stays simplistically the same.

Having the type of ministry that I do, there have been times that I have experienced much opposition from the kingdom of darkness. In fact, I have learned to take it as an encouragement. If the enemy is upset with me to such an extent that he goes out of his way in an attempt to sway me from my path, then I must be doing something right. However, it is understanding where we stand in authority in the spirit realm which determines the effect that such attacks will have on us.

I remember a while back there was a woman who was deeply involved in the occult who sought me out. I still, to this day, do not know how she found out where I lived. She was disturbed by what I was doing for the kingdom of God, and wanted to place a curse and hex upon me.

Now, as I say this, I want to clarify something: Not everyone who is involved in the occult is trying to intentionally advance the kingdom of darkness. Many are involved in such things because they are curious about the supernatural. They are looking for God, and as a result turn to spiritual things. Due to a lack of discernment, they look to spiritual things that are both perverted and corrupt. However, there are people out there who are deeply entwined in the occult, who have dedicated their lives to stopping the movement of the Spirit of God on the earth. This woman was such a person.

When this woman sought me out, the moment she laid eyes on me, she immediately began speaking out a demonic curse over my life. For those who do not understand their identity and authority, this might come across as frightening, but when we understand who we are, we know that the enemy's vile words cannot take root in our lives unless we permit them to. Remember, the enemy has some power, but you have authority. You are the one in control. The enemy's head is under your foot, not the other way around.

As she was speaking, I asked the Spirit of God what He wanted me to do. He responded saying, "I want you to begin to worship me."

Obeying, right in front of this woman, I closed my eyes, held out my hands and began to thank Jesus for His goodness. After a few minutes of doing this, the tangibility of the glory of God began to increase around us. It increased until I could hear that the woman who came to curse me was weeping. This woman who came to me with the intention of cursing me had begun to encounter the heart of God in that moment. I then reached out my arm to place my hand on her shoulder. Right then and there she accepted the Lord into her heart. This woman, right in that moment, was translated out of the kingdom of darkness, and straight into the kingdom of light.

Often what we do with spiritual warfare, is if the attack seems big, then we assume that the answer to the attack must be big as well. We complicate spiritual matters by trying to interpret them with human wisdom. Just because the problem seems complicated does not mean that the solution has to be as well. No matter how big or small an attack is, the enemy's strategy of warfare is to sway you in the perspective of how you view yourself and how you view God. It sounds simple, because it is.

If satan's priority in warfare towards Jesus had to do with swaying Him from His sonship, we know that a powerful tool in standing upright in the midst of a spiritual war is holding on to what the Father has spoken over us. We need to allow ourselves to be saturated in the Father's blessing, knowing that what He says about us is true. This is where Adam and Eve failed. They could not prevent the serpent from whispering lies in their minds. They were not to blame for the warfare that they experienced. However, they failed because they did not go to the Father in intimacy and friendship, allowing Him to speak into them to dethrone the lies from their minds. Instead, they shut themselves off from the Father, meditating on head knowledge until it became heart knowledge.

Romans 12:2: "And do not be conformed to this world, but be transformed by the renewing of your mind, that you may prove what is that good and acceptable and perfect will of God."

Ever since we were birthed into existence, the enemy has tried to tell us that we are orphans. He has tried to trick us into believing that we have no Father. This is why we are often so swayed by spiritual attacks. Instead of responding in confidence as sons and daughters of God, we become swayed, because at times we have placed more faith in what the enemy is saying compared to what the Father is saying. We become reeds flapping in the wind rather than solid pillars. This is why we need to renew our minds in what the Father is saying. We cannot just hear Him speak and then forget about it. We need to diligently meditate on what God the Father is saying, to the point that it becomes a part of who we are.

So what does this practically look like while experiencing this form of external warfare, no matter the degree of attack? Let us learn from Adam and Eve's mistake. If the enemy plants a lie in our mind, we cannot take ownership of what the enemy is saying. We cannot pull it into our heart. We need to take this to intimacy with God the Father. We need to turn to Him to receive His word, which dethrones all lies. So if you are in a situation where the enemy is igniting things such as insecurity, anxiety or fear, do not dwell on those things. Our mindsets are fashioned in the image of what we allow ourselves to dwell and meditate on. Turn to the Father heart of God and ask Him what He says about you. When He speaks, begin to meditate on the Father's word so that His truth can chase away the lie.

Stepping into intimacy with God in this way can look different to different individuals. If the enemy is whispering lies to you, it might be beneficial for you to simply ask the Father what the truth is. For others it may look like turning on worship music, to engage the heart of God through music. It could look like opening your Bible to meditate on the truth of the written Word of God. It could also look like going for a drive with God to reflect on past prophetic words that have been spoken over you, which are in contrast to the lies that the enemy is pressing on you. There is no structure to intimacy with the Lord, because He is so relational that He wants His relationship with you to be unique from everyone else's. The important thing is that you abide in Him to commune with the Father heart of God towards you.

When we renew our minds based on what the Father has spoken over us, His love and truth becomes established in our hearts. The enemy's lies cannot penetrate His love and truth. Eventually, you reach a place where you simply shrug off the warfare when it begins to wage against your mind, because it cannot exist in the culture that God has established in your inner-man. You become un-penetrable, because Jesus the Rock becomes solidified in your understanding of your identity as a son or daughter of God.

Throughout this chapter, I have shared a story concerning basic external warfare and extreme external warfare. As I mentioned before, even though the expression of warfare can be diverse, the objective is always the same. Whether you are having thoughts that are demonically influenced penetrating your mind, experiencing fear in the nighttime, or are experiencing demonically influenced words through others, it is all under your feet as a son or daughter of God. Do not let anyone trick you into forgetting that.

Reform your mind in the truth of the Word of God and in what God the Father says about you. This is how you can live your life not feeling as though you are struggling towards victory, but are reigning and influencing from victory.

Practical Warfare

Previously, I discussed that the enemy has no *authority* whatsoever in our lives because of the cross. However, I also mentioned that the enemy does have *power*. When we do not allow Jesus to be Lord over different aspects of our lives, we give the enemy a right to influence us in those areas. This can occur in a variety of ways. Before we get into some of the heavier things concerning internal warfare, I want to talk a bit about the more practical side of spiritual warfare. Often, we do not realize that what we do in the natural realm can influence what happens in the spirit realm, and how it affects us.

Psalm 91:4: "He (the Father) shall cover you with His feathers, and under His wings you shall take refuge; His truth shall be your shield and buckler."

God's word over us is that He will cover us

with His wings. He will be our refuge. However, we need to understand that it is a personal choice whether or not we allow ourselves to abide under His wings. A few verses down, in Psalm 91:9, it says that we can experience God as our refuge, "because you have made the LORD, who *is* my refuge, even the Most High, your dwelling place".

See, we have a personal responsibility to make God our dwelling place. God has provided a place for us to be sheltered under His wings, but we have to choose to dwell there instead of standing outside of His abode and the shade of His covering. If we are not willing to make Him our dwelling place in the different areas of our lives then we could be living outside of God's covering, making us vulnerable to spiritual warfare.

There has been a lie that we have embraced in the church for years, saying that Jesus has done everything, so therefore we do not need to do anything. Jesus has certainly accomplished everything. However, we need to understand that in order for us to step into the fullness of His accomplishment, we need to co-labour with Him by taking up personal responsibility. We need to remember that God always honours our free will. That means that through the cross, all of the blessings are ours to feast upon (Ephesians 1:3). However, God will not force us to feast upon them. We can still choose to experience less than what our birthright makes available to us.

Have you ever wondered why God placed the tree of the knowledge of good and evil in the garden with Adam and Eve? In the wisdom of man this would seem like foolishness. Adam and Eve lived in a personal paradise, being allowed to continuously feast upon the love of God and the culture of heaven. Yet, God put this tree, which had the potential to ruin everything for them, in the middle of the garden. God placed this tree in Eden, not to tempt Adam and Eve, but because He honours free will. He wanted to give them complete access to experience fullness with Him, as well as the option to choose not to. True love does not trap people.

This is the same opportunity that God gives us. We have the opportunity to walk in the full benefits of the cross. We can bring every area under submission to Christ, to encounter His intimate love in every realm of who we are, or we can compartmentalize ourselves, allowing Him into some areas, but not all. He gives us this liberty because He loves us enough to give us free will. However, when you have truly encountered the friendship of God, I do not know how you could choose anything over and above being in relationship with Him in every aspect of who you are.

Now let's look at some of the practical areas of our lives that we can bring into alignment with Him:

We know that Biblically it is God's will that we walk in perfect health in Him. We know that Isaiah 53:5 says:

"He (Jesus) was wounded for our transgressions, He was bruised for our iniquities; The chastisement for our peace was upon Him, and by His stripes we are healed."

I do not believe that sickness and disease are from God. I know that the enemy's primary strategy to hinder the body, which is the temple of the Lord, is to inflict sickness and disease. However, we need to understand that there is a level of co-labouring necessary to stay healthy.

Before I was in full time ministry, I was a full time construction worker. I went from being in an extremely demanding physical job, to a job in ministry that was fully demanding emotionally and spiritually. Stepping into ministry, I did not have the knowledge or wisdom to know that because my jobs were so different, I would have to take care of my body in a different way as well. Almost immediately after entering full time ministry, I gained about 60 pounds. I was amazed at how this effected my life, especially when I would travel for itinerant ministry. I was constantly fatigued whenever I would travel anywhere for ministry. Even while I was up on stage speaking, I noticed how my weariness would often hinder me from ministering out of a place of passion.

We are responsible for taking care of our bodies on the earth, which enables us to step into the full blessing of the health that Jesus paid for on the cross. If I am eating fast food every day and not stewarding my body well, then I am not doing my part to co-labour in this area of my life to see this promise come to pass (1 Corinthians 6:19-20). This of course, is not to say that every time we face troubles in our body, it is caused by our lack of stewardship. This could not be further from the truth. I have met many individuals who have treated their body extremely well, yet experienced external warfare in their health. However, in my case, when I was not willing to co-labour with God in the area of my health, I was not allowing myself to step under the shelter of the Father's wings in this area of my life. I was actually giving the enemy a foothold in my body to attack me in my health. See, there are times where the enemy is simply waging warfare externally. However, there are other times when it is in our control to prevent him from having access to our lives. Sometimes it is something that we are doing, or not doing, in the realm of the natural that is opening doors for the demonic in the spirit realm.

God brought me on a journey, training me on kingdom health. I changed my eating patterns drastically, which meant that when I would travel for ministry, I would make special meal requests. It is difficult to describe how excruciating it was at times, when all the guest speakers from a conference were together, waiting for a meal, and out would come a pizza for dinner. Everyone else would happily scarf it down as I would sit there politely with my green salad. Most of you reading this have probably heard of the Five Love Languages. Well, I believe that there are actually six love languages, because my love language is pizza. However, I knew that if I wanted to be in it for the long haul, and see the fullness of my calling fulfilled, I needed to change my lifestyle. I ended up losing all of the weight and was able to cultivate a lifestyle of healthy eating, closing the door in the spirit realm for the enemy to attack my body.

Another area where many experience practical warfare is in the realm of finances. I have met many in the church who are primarily attacked in this area. There are times when we experience external attacks because the enemy does not want us to be blessed. However, sometimes we can bring financial warfare upon ourselves simply by being opposed to receiving financial wisdom. Learning how to make a budget could save many of us from plenty of financial warfare. Gaining an understanding that it is not God's heart for us to be in debt could shut the enemy out of our financial lives. A lack of personal responsibility and an unwillingness to learn basic life skills could often cause us to miss God's blessing.

I am going to say something, and I do not want you to become offended. Are you ready for it? Here it is: Sometimes we are waiting for a huge financial miracle, for our debt to be cancelled, or for $80,000 to miraculously appear in our bank account. Believe me, God does these things. I have some financial testimonies that would rock your socks off. However, sometimes we need to understand that if we do not carry financial wisdom when we receive such a blessing, that gift could actually become a stumbling block to us instead of a blessing.

I have met people who have had God miraculously cancel great sums of debt, but because they were not willing to grow in practical financial skills, they ended up in more debt a few years afterwards. This is why, when people ask me to pray for them for financial increase and breakthrough, I often make it a priority to pray for them to receive wisdom together with their financial blessing. I believe that there are actually times when God withholds blessing because we have not aligned ourselves practically with wisdom, knowing that large sums of money coming to us would hurt us more than benefit us. Does this mean that God does not want to bless us? Absolutely not. What it does mean is that we need to be willing to allow God to reform our minds in how we view finances. We need to position ourselves as good stewards so that God can entrust us with blessing. He does not want our finances to have authority over us. He wants to train us in wisdom to instead walk in authority and control over our finances. When this happens, we are able to comprehend that money is not our master, but is a tool to advance God's kingdom.

Relationships are another area where we could save ourselves the burden of unnecessary warfare if we are willing to learn the necessary life skills. If we are not willing to develop communication skills and learn how to handle conflict in a healthy way, this could give the enemy opportunity to bring strife through our relationships. I am not going to try to lay out a teaching on relationships right now. There are already many great books and resources available regarding how we can healthily relate to one another. However, I would encourage anyone who has not already done so, to read some books on healthy communication and learn how to honour others in the context of relationships. I would also encourage you to pick up some resources relating to what healthy boundaries should look like in the realm of relationships.

Whether it is through our health, our finances, our relationships, or any other aspect of life, we need to see how the supernatural and the practical are supposed to blend together in us. I would go as far as to say that in order to walk in a place of maturity as a spiritual person, we need to be a place where both the supernatural and the practical are married.

Before I was in full time ministry, I thought that in order to have a successful ministry all that I would need to do is know how to teach well, how to prophesy accurately and have enough faith to see the sick healed. Now that I am in ministry, I understand that even if I can do those three things extremely well, if I do not have a focus on administration then I will not be able to impact as many people with these gifts. There is an aspect of moving in the Spirit which is completely supernatural, yet there is another side that is tremendously practical as well. I need to know how to prophesy, as well as how to keep on top of bookings for speaking engagements. I need to know how to pray for the sick, as well as having good people skills in order to come across well when interacting with other leaders around the world. If I were not willing to continually grow in my faith for the supernatural as well as in my life skills in ministry, it would give the enemy a huge foothold that would affect the impact that I now get to make for the advancement of the kingdom of heaven. In fact, I have met many people who have a great call to minister to the masses, both in the church and in the marketplace. These are people who have been greatly gifted by God, but because of a lack of willingness to grow in practical life skills, their level of influence is drastically minimized.

As we allow God into each of these areas, we step under His hedge of protection (Job 1:10). God is raising us up to make kingdom decisions for our lives. I have often said that Holy Spirit takes us from our orphan mentalities to show us that we are sons and daughters of God. He then takes us as sons and daughters to teach us how to be fathers and mothers. Holy Spirit then takes us and refines us to be kings and queens, training us to make royal decisions for our lives.

I am going to take you through a time of repentance. God's heart is that every aspect of who we are would be brought into alignment with His will. God the Father wants you to experience the fullness of His love in every realm of your life. If you want to bring different practical realms of your life into alignment with the kingdom of God, then feel free to pray this with me.

"Father God, I repent for the different areas of my life that I have not stewarded well. I call on wisdom to invade my life, that I may know how to properly co-labour with You, Lord. I give You my body, Lord. I invite You to teach me practical tools so that I will experience the full blessing of kingdom health. I invite You into my mind, my will and my emotions. I invite You to teach me kingdom-life skills. I give You my mentality concerning finances, Lord. Bring alignment and purity in how I view money. Help me to see it not as a master, but as a tool to advance Your kingdom. I pray for alignment in my relationships Lord. I ask You for communication skills and the ability to know how to approach and handle kingdom conflict. Teach me to honour. Teach me how to not take offense with others. I do not want to hold back any aspect of who I am from You. Come and reign with the fullness of who You are, in the fullness of who I am."

Internal Warfare

Now, let's look at a form of warfare that is less practical and more emotional. We are going to examine what warfare looks like when it is not our circumstances being attacked, but instead, our soul experiencing the battle. Our soul includes our mind, our will and our emotions. Whereas practical warfare is about us having holes in our life skills, internal warfare occurs when the enemy has a foothold in an area of our soul.

To start off unpacking the subject of internal warfare, I am going to share with you a personal story to use as a teaching parable:

I am going to be completely honest with you. I am not perfect. Are you surprised? You shouldn't be. We often place an unrealistic expectation on leaders in the church just because they are the ones on a stage with the microphone. This is an expectation that I refuse to submit to. Just because I speak in public and have written books does not mean that I do not have times when I feel insecure. It also does not mean that I do not have times when I feel anxious. Is it God's will that I experience insecurity and anxiety? Absolutely not. However, we are all on a journey, and God calls us to embrace the process, not to run from it.

I do not often share from my childhood. It is not because I do not want to share my full testimony, but because I do not want to dishonour those from my past who were instrumental in sparking different forms of trauma in my life. There were aspects of it that were amazing, but other parts that were highly dysfunctional. I will leave it at that.

When I gave my heart to the Lord at 16 years of age, I was oblivious to the internal trauma that had been forming in me over a number of years. Part of the reason was because I had suppressed it. The other part was due to the fact that young men often are not in tune with the fullness of their own emotions until they hit their 20's. I was about 21 when the years of torment and trauma caught up with me and I began showing signs of Post Traumatic Stress Disorder (PTSD).

The PTSD would manifest itself in the form of extreme anxiety attacks, which were often triggered in group settings. I would be with a group of people when, all of a sudden, out of nowhere irrational fear would spark in my emotions. I would have to leave because I would literally be trembling in fear. It would take a great amount of time by myself to calm down again and be able to step into a right state of mind. The anxiety would also be triggered while asleep at times. If I would suddenly wake up in the night, it would be enough to spin me into a panic attack for hours. To top it all off, I was struggling with this anxiety while pastoring. A pastor's job in the church is to take care of people, bring healing to the broken hearted and to build community. This was certainly by no means an easy task to build community when the anxiety I experienced was triggered in group settings.

My wife and I were very perplexed, wondering what we should do about what I was experiencing. The obvious answer was to go through some inner healing sessions. I went through a few sessions in faith, believing that God would deliver me from my trauma. Each time I went through a session, the anxiety attacks would return a few days afterwards. Then I tried going through counselling. This again, brought no change whatsoever. My wife and I knew that we just needed to keep believing for my freedom. We kept saying "yes" to Jesus every single day. This was not a short journey. I believed for my freedom for years. Once I realized the severity of what I was going through, I began to understand that I had been experiencing these symptoms on a smaller scale for much longer than I had thought. I had struggled with them for years even before I met my wife. However, when we regularly live in a form of dysfunction, we become familiar with it. We even begin to think that our anxiety or insecurities are simply a part of our personality. The PTSD attacks were amplified and at their peak for the entire three years that I pastored.

Shortly after I finished my time pastoring, my wife had gone away on a trip and I was sitting on the couch, playing guitar and spending time with the Lord. As I strummed away, I felt Holy Spirit speak to me. He said, "My goodness is going to pass before you tonight."

I didn't even know what that meant, but was extremely excited. All of a sudden, I saw something out of the corner of my eye. I looked to the other end of the couch and Jesus was sitting there. This was not a "receive it by faith" type of experience. Jesus was actually sitting on the couch with me. The moment I saw Him, a swell of emotion hit me. I immediately felt a desire to go for a drive, which is something I often do in my intimate times to connect with God.

I was sitting in my car, driving with Jesus sitting next to me. The deep emotion I felt in that moment was like nothing I had ever experienced before. I could feel the deep places within my soul begin to open up, areas of my heart and emotions that I hadn't known even existed. I had never before allowed anyone into these areas of my life. I wept uncontrollably and Jesus wept with me. He entered those areas of my soul. This drive with Jesus lasted about 2 hours. He shared with me things that evening that, to this day, I have not shared with anyone.

I am pleased to say that ever since that evening, I haven't had a single anxiety attack. One touch from God can heal your broken heart. I believe in counselling and inner healing sessions whole-heartedly, but one God-ordained moment with Him can accomplish more than 20 years of counselling.

This story is the perfect example of internal warfare. The enemy was not trying to simply plant thoughts in my head in order to get into my heart. He already had a foothold in my heart, which essentially gave him permission to torment me in this realm of my life. Without realizing it, I had not allowed Jesus to reign in that area of my soul. This in turn allowed the enemy to hold me in a mentality of orphanship, preventing me from experiencing the love of God in this area of my life. It was not until I allowed Jesus in, that the warfare ceased to exist.

If we are experiencing a time of warfare and

the enemy is blatantly attacking us, it would be wise for us discern whether it is an external attack, or whether we have allowed the enemy to have free reign in an area of our lives. It is important for us to discern properly because how we respond depends on whether it is internal or external warfare. If you are experiencing an external attack, the enemy is trying to trick you into believing that you are an orphan. If it is an internal attack, a part of you already believes that you are an orphan. There is a distinct difference.

We need to come to a place like Jesus was when He said in John 14:30: "The ruler of this world (the enemy) is coming, and he has nothing in Me." We need to allow Jesus to have full reign in every aspect of our being, that the enemy will have no hold in us.

To be honest with you, I do not overly enjoy making personal stories public. However, I believe that being a leader means actually going before others to lead them. If I want to encourage you to be vulnerable with God concerning deep and guarded issues that may be in your heart, then as a leader, I need to be willing to model that vulnerability to you.

Since we are all on a journey, we are constantly in the process of allowing Jesus to reign within the entirety of our beings. Many of us have wounds concerning different anxieties, insecurities and fears. We have a responsibility to not dismiss these things as part of our personalities. We need to see them for what they are. They are heart wounds. It is not God's will for us to be stuck in heart wounds. Period. We need to keep allowing the love of God to fill us until there is no place for the enemy anymore. Walking in wholeness in Christ is a journey.

I know there are times when we genuinely want Jesus to bring breakthrough in the realm of the soul, but the victory has not yet materialized itself, much like the story I just shared. I persevered for years without seeing a change. If this is the case, then we need to keep holding onto the promise of God that we will walk in full freedom. Do not give up. Do not grow weary. God's will is for you to be free.

There are also times when we stubbornly hold onto pain, whether we realize we are doing it or not. We need to understand that just because the pain is familiar to us, it does not mean that it is safe. You have a unique calling and purpose over your life, and it would be a shame for you to not step into it because of an unwilling heart. We need to let Jesus in, and let the pain and offense go.

Moses was probably one of the greatest leaders in all of history, and is my favourite person in the Old Testament who I feel that I personally relate to the best. However, all of us make mistakes because none of us are perfect, other than Jesus of course. If you remember correctly, when God first commissioned Moses into his calling as a leader to help deliver Israel in Exodus 3, he was insecure in walking out his mandate. Moses feared that God could not use him because he could not speak with eloquence. He had a heart wound. At some point in Moses' life he had embraced a lie about himself believing that God could not use him to lead because of his speech impediment. God gave Moses the option to confront his wound; He said "Go, and I will be with your mouth and teach you what you shall say" (Exodus 4:12). Instead of dealing with his heart issue by trusting God, he had asked God to send someone else. God counteracted by permitting Aaron to be Moses' mouthpiece.

Since Moses was unwilling to deal with his internal wound, he was inviting the enemy to have a foothold within his soul to wage war, creating an internal battle. Since Moses did not face his insecurity with his speech impediment while he was in the secret place with God, he had to fight his inner battle everyday as he walked as the leader of a nation.

After Moses had walked as the leader of Israel for a few years, God asked him to do something that triggered his insecurity. The Israelites had run out of water and began to ask God to provide for them. God spoke to Moses and told him to speak to a rock, causing water to flow from it (Numbers 20:8). Moses had to either trust God that He would give him the ability to speak or he would have to compromise God's will because he was afraid. Instead of speaking to the rock, Moses hit it with his staff because insecurity dictated his decision. This was not a small matter in God's eyes. Moses had disobeyed the Lord and was not permitted to enter the Promised Land because of it.

We can see how Moses' wound stood in direct conflict with his promise and destiny. Moses' inability to let God reign in his soul gave the enemy a right to wage war internally, which eventually manifested in external consequences. We need to stop running from our hurts, wounds and pasts. God has proven that He can be trusted. It is time to let Him in.

Often, we view our heart wounds as daunting mountains that seem nearly impossible to overcome. When we see a heart wound for what it is, we understand that we often work them up to be bigger than they actually are. A heart wound is simply a lie that we have embraced about ourselves. Lies such as this can be rooted in our hearts in a variety of different ways. For example, if you faced a form of abandonment growing up, it would be easy to believe the lie that you are not lovable. Or if you have experienced forms or sexual or physical abuse growing up, then it may taint your perception of seeing yourself as valuable or precious in the sight of God. For those who grew up in poverty, it may be easy to believe that God does not want to provide for you. The possibilities of different experiences sparking lies in our soul is virtually endless. However, something we need to remember is that, no matter what has happened to you throughout your life, the pain is rooted in a lie, and this lie is trying to convince you that you are not loved. It is trying to convince you that you are alone, which could not be further from the truth.

One of the reasons why a heart wound seems so daunting is because we have built our habits and thought patterns around these wounds. We have accommodated to them for years by weaving our lives around our insecurities and fears. What we need to understand is that overcoming a wound is simply re-patterning our minds to stop believing the lie we have embraced, and replacing it with the truth that God is declaring over us.

As we are receiving healing in our soul, it does not have to look like us struggling to climb the mighty mountain of inner healing. Instead, it can look like soaring on the wings of the Lord by trusting that what He says about you is truth.

I want to share another story with you, which I believe draws an interesting parable for us concerning inner healing. Approximately 8 years ago, I was at a soaking meeting with a group of friends. If you don't know what a soaking meeting is, it is where you get together with others and spend time "soaking" in God's presence together. While doing this, you spend time listening to the Lord, and share what God showed you while spending time in His presence.

During the soaking time, I was laying on the ground with my eyes closed. All of a sudden, I began seeing a picture in my mind's eye. In the vision, it looked like I was sitting cross-legged on a grassy field in heaven. Across from me sat God the Father. As I looked at Him, I was mesmerized by His face. His face shone as bright as the sun. In fact, it shone so bright that I could not distinguish any facial features.

All of a sudden, a question sparked in my heart. Trying my best to look straight at the Father's glowing face, I said to Him, "Father, what do I look like?"

Reaching behind His back, He pulled out a mirror and held it before me. As I looked in the mirror to see my reflection, I saw that my face shone the same as His did. We need to always remember that we are created in the image of God.

As the vision ended, our time of soaking ended as well. I sat up from the floor and looked over to one of my friends. When I looked over, she immediately screamed. Confused, I turned to another friend of mine. When she saw my face, she began to weep. I asked them why they had such strong reactions and they told me that it was because my face was physically shining.

When you look in the mirror, what do you see? What perception do you look at yourself through? Do you perceive yourself through the lens of your past? Do you see yourself through the lens of what others expect of you? Do you see yourself as lovable? As significant? If not, then you may be seeing yourself through the lens of a heart wound. God the Father wants to train your eyes to see yourself from His perspective. He wants your confidence to reflect your true identity. Your heavenly Father wants to free you from the torment of self-hatred.

I want to take some time now to lead you into receiving freedom in your heart. As I mentioned earlier in this chapter, the reason for sharing my personal story of freedom was to model vulnerability to you, so that you will know that you can be vulnerable with Father God. He wants to begin to bring healing to you right now. He wants to touch your heart. He wants you to truly see yourself the way He sees you. Since receiving my own emotional breakthrough in the realm of the soul, I have seen many others receive instant healing and freedom from lifelong traumas while sitting under my ministry. As I guide you through this process, you may very well receive an instant and dramatic inner healing. For others, God may give you a smaller breakthrough. This may be only the beginning of a journey where you allow Jesus to come in to bring healing to your soul. No matter what level of freedom you receive, I am tremendously excited for what God is doing in your heart.

I want to lead you in asking God some questions. So right now, I want you to quiet your mind and bring your heart into a posture to receive what God has for you. The first series of questions is going to consist of you asking God questions concerning who He is. The second series of questions consists of you asking questions about who you are. Take time on this part. The first question you are going to ask Him is this:

"Father God, is there a lie that I am believing about who You are?"

Take time waiting on Him. Remember, if we are viewing God as distant, unemotional or angry, then our perception of Him is not correct.

Once you feel that you hear God answer, ask Him this:

"Father, is there anyone who has contributed to my false perception of You?"

God may bring someone to mind. Often the way we view God the Father will parallel experiences that we have had in past relationships. For example, if you were rejected by an authority figure in your life who you looked up to, you may view God the Father as someone who would reject you. If God has brought someone to mind, then I would like to lead you through a prayer of forgiveness. This is crucial to step into our healing. When we do not forgive, we are holding ourselves in a place of bitterness, which prevents us from stepping into full freedom.

Pray this with me:

"*Father, I choose to forgive (fill in the blank with name) for contributing to the lie I have believed about who You are. I choose to release the offense in my heart towards this person, that I may see them the way You see them.*"

As you prayed this prayer of forgiveness, you may or may not have felt genuine in your emotions. Something we need to remember is that forgiveness is not an emotion. It is a choice. This means that you may not feel it in your heart to forgive, but by practicing self-control, you can choose to view this person through the lens of forgiveness that God sees them through. Forgiveness can be a process, so if you continue to feel bitterness when this person comes to mind, continue to walk in self-control and make the decision to forgive them.

Now, ask God this question:

"Father God, who is it that You say You are?"

Once God answers this question, you are going to begin to ask God about yourself. Ask Him this:

"Father is there a lie that I am believing about myself?"

Once you feel that you hear God answer, ask Him this:

"Father, is there anyone who has contributed to my false perception of myself?"

If God brings someone to mind then pray this prayer:

"Father, I choose to forgive (fill in the blank with name) for contributing to the lie I have believed about myself. I choose to release the offense in my heart towards this person, that I may see them the way that You see them."

Now ask God this final question:

"Father, who is it that You say I am?"

Different people will often feel a variety of different things emotionally after going through a process like this. You may feel a bit lighter because God has brought healing and clarity. Or you may be feeling a bit raw because God was bringing up deep emotional things for you. You may also feel a bit heavy because God has surfaced some things in your soul that He will be walking you through for the next while. It is impossible to reduce what God does to a formula because He is not mechanical, but organic. He is so ravished by you that He will journey differently in relationship with you than anyone else.

You are the apple of God's eye and the greatest desire of His heart. He is happy with you and smiles over you. You are precious and priceless to Him. He sees you as beautiful. You were created with a brilliant mind. Your Father God is proud of you and believes in your dreams.

You are special.

You are significant.

You are loved.

Practical Tips to Maintain Healing

There are certain keys I would like to give you in order to walk out your healing. Just as the enemy has tactics to keep us in a state of internal warfare, he also has tactics to pull us back into our old wounds. Therefore, it is beneficial for us to understand how to maintain our healing.

When we are wounded in the soul, it often looks like this: To build a house, you must always start with the foundation. Because of the foundation's importance, it is very crucial to take the necessary time to build it, much like how in our lives, God takes much time forming confidence in our identity in Him. When we are wounded, it is as though we have a cracked, uneven foundation instead of one that is solid and unblemished. When we build our habits and life patterns on a wounded foundation, whatever we build will also be uneven and flawed.

Often, when we receive healing in the realm of the soul, the cracks in the foundation have been healed up, but the habits and life patterns that were built upon those wounds still remain. Sometimes God will instantly remove the habits together with the wound. However, if there are unhealthy habits that do remain, we need to learn how to re-pattern the way we live, so that we live out of a place of wholeness instead of old patterns of dysfunction. If we do not learn how to tear down or adjust these habits and life patterns, the enemy could use them to re-spark a wound.

For the sake of giving you clarity, I will give you an example. Many people who struggle with fear of rejection also struggle with isolation. They isolate themselves because they fear that if they are close to people they will be rejected. So, instead of attempting to be close to others in relationship, they withdraw in an attempt to escape the pain that potential rejection could cause. The fear of rejection is the wound, and isolation is the unhealthy life pattern built upon the wound. Now, let's say that a person who has a deep fear of rejection is healed of their fear. The fear and cracks in the foundation may be gone, but there may still be a lingering, unhealthy habit of withdrawing from people. They may not isolate out of fear, but because it is familiar to them. By not changing this habit they could very well reignite loneliness, reactivating a fear of rejection all over again. This has the potential to create a constant unhealthy cycle, causing the person to be stuck in their wound. This is why it is important to focus on changing our lifestyle instead of always looking for the quick fix.

It is much the same as looking at weight loss. Do you know why extreme diets do not normally work? It is because these diets are all about trying to promote a quick fix, instead of training on a healthy lifestyle. Even for those who do lose a lot of extra body weight, without the knowledge of how to walk out your health in a lifestyle, most end up gaining all of the weight back.

Tearing down and readjusting old habits does not need to be a strenuous process. We can simply take it back to intimacy with the Lord. When Jesus as a child asked the Pharisees questions in the temple, He was modelling for us that it is wise to ask questions (Luke 2:46-47). Ask Holy Spirit questions. He is not intimidated by them. When we ask God questions, we are positioning ourselves as students, and giving Him authority to be our Teacher. If you have received healing in the realm of the soul, then simply ask the Lord if there are any unhealthy habits or life patterns that you need to change. If the Lord shows you anything, begin to ask Him for strategies to partner with Him to change those habits.

While going through this process, it would also be healthy to have people around you who you know and trust, to speak into your life to bring guidance. Proverbs 15:22 says, "Without counsel, plans go awry, but in the multitude of counsellors they are established." God has created us to be in relationship. Sometimes when you are experiencing warfare you cannot always realistically trust yourself. Often when going through a time of warfare, our emotions can cloud our discernment. In these times, it is greatly beneficial for others who are not emotionally attached to your situation to give you guidance and counsel, because they will be able to see things that you cannot.

There is also great wisdom in asking the Lord what your triggers are, so that you know how to avoid the things that could re-trigger a wound. If we are to look back to the example of fear of rejection, it may be a trigger from a past wound to spend an unhealthy amount of time by yourself. Therefore, you know you should not isolate yourself. Another example would be if you have been delivered from an addiction to alcohol. Would it be a trigger to hang out with your friends at a pub? If so, then you should eliminate the possibility of this trigger by not allowing yourself to be in that environment.

Even in cases where God does very quick inner healing, there still needs to be an awareness of our own personal responsibility in walking out the healing. In my case of receiving healing from PTSD, even though I no longer had anxiety attacks, there were still times when I would feel anxiety. If I did not continue to commune with God through those times of anxious feelings, then those small doses of anxiety could have very well ignited a panic attack, reactivating a heart wound.

When we receive an inner healing from God, the warfare moves from internal to external warfare. The enemy knows that he has lost ground, so will try to attack your mind again to get back into your heart.

I have a friend who was miraculously delivered from a seven year addiction to pornography. Once she was delivered, she began to have dreams about pornography. This left her feeling confused, as she knew in her heart that she had been delivered. However, the tormenting dreams made her question whether or not she had actually been delivered.

The enemy likes to attack you externally in such a way in order to try to trick you into believing that you have not received healing at all. He does this by attacking you with a lie in your mind similar to what God has already freed you from in your heart. I have met many people who would be completely freed from a specific heart wound, yet a few days or a week later, they would begin to feel emotions that they had been feeling before they were set free. Then they would start slipping into the lie that they had lost, or had never received the healing that God had brought.

This is one of the reasons why it is so important for us to be transformed by the renewing of our minds in what the Father is saying. In these types of scenarios, we may have believed these lies for 20 years before we were set free. That means that you have 20 years of experience believing that you are an orphan in that area of your heart, and now you are trying to reform yourself to know that you are a son or daughter of God. There may be times when you view yourself through an incorrect lens, as it is a habit to view yourself that way. This does not mean that you have lost your healing. It means that you are now learning to renew your mind.

Some of you who have gone through this chapter may have received profound healing in your heart. Although I have provided some good tools to maintain your healing, the greatest tool that I can teach you is to continually allow yourself to fall deeper in love with God. He loves you unconditionally and His desire is for you. Continue to allow the Father heart of God to consume you. I am going to pray a prayer over you:

"Father God, I thank You for the healing that You have brought to Your child's heart. I thank You that You love them. I thank You that they are significant to You. Right now I declare that what You have deposited in their hearts is sealed in the blood of Jesus. I thank You that You will finish the good work that You have started in them. Continue to show them how special they are to You."

A Royal Commission

God is raising up a mighty army. This army will co-labour with Jesus to dismantle the kingdom of darkness with the kingdom of heaven. You are a part of this mighty army. You are not disqualified in any way, shape or form from moving in the things of God, or from bringing healing to the world. Many have disqualified themselves from being used by God because they have allowed their current or past circumstances to dictate how much of an impact they make for God.

Scripture shows us that many of Jesus' disciples rejected Him right before He was crucified. Two of the most well-known disciples who rejected Him were Peter and Judas. When faced with the possibility of persecution, Peter denied Jesus three times (Matthew 26:69-75). Judas, out of greed in his heart, betrayed Jesus to those who crucified Him (Luke 22:47-48).

Now, there is something here I want to point out to you. Since Peter had a revelation of the grace Jesus offered, he did not consider himself disqualified from the kingdom of God after he had rejected Jesus. Even though Peter blatantly rejected Him, Jesus simply restored Peter as a man and as a leader. In fact, Jesus made Peter the lead apostle of the 12 apostles. Judas' response when he rejected Jesus was very different. When he sinned against the Son of Man, he disqualified himself within his heart from ever being used for the purposes of God, and committed suicide by hanging himself on a tree (Matthew 27:5). It is interesting that Judas hung himself on a tree. This provides a powerful prophetic picture of how Judas did not believe that the sacrifice of Jesus hanging and dying on the cross (a tree) for his sin was enough for him to be redeemed. So, in a sense, Judas crucified his own self for his sin.

Unfortunately, this is a viewpoint that many have adopted. Because of our current or past circumstances, in our hearts we disqualify ourselves from being used by God. Therefore we submit to a form of spiritual death by believing that we are not worth being used. Realistically, we need to understand that Jesus would have treated Judas in the same way He treated Peter. I truly believe in my heart that if Judas had been repentant and had understood the power of the cross, Jesus simply would have restored him as a man and a leader. I do not believe that it was God's primary will for Mathias to fill Judas' role as an apostle for the church of Acts. I believe that it was God's will to restore Judas to a place of wholeness.

My friend, if you have ever felt like the last choice, then you are the perfect candidate to do remarkable things for God's kingdom. God has a reputation for picking those who feel like they are nothing. He picks them, befriends them, and turns them into someone powerful. He is there for us throughout the whole story of our lives. He chooses us in our weakness and refines us to be strong in Him. He calls us when we are dependent on ourselves and others, and teaches us to be dependent on Him. I am so thankful that God chose Peter the coward, and turned him into Peter the apostle. I am so thankful that God called Matthew the tax collector, and turned him into an apostle and author of one of the gospels. God chose Moses the murderer, and turned him into a man who delivered a nation. God chose David the adulterer, and made him one of the greatest kings who ever lived. Many do not know this, but the prophet Daniel was actually a eunuch, which was one of the most disregarded statuses in his time (Daniel 1:6-10). Yet, God raised him up to be one of the most profound prophets in the Old Testament. God chooses the least likely and uses them to do what does not seem possible (1 Corinthians 1:27).

It has been an honour journeying with you. I hope that you are beginning to understand your importance in the kingdom of God, and in the

Father's heart. From a place of victory, and from the place of knowing that you are loved, you are called to bring great change. You are called to influence not only the physical world around you, but the invisible realm as well. You are chosen by God to reign in authority with Him on the earth. No strategy or plan of the enemy can stop you, as you abide in the abode of the love of God.

You are more important than you realize. You are so important that the Creator of the universe became a man, so that your heart could be reconciled to His. He did this because He desires to be in relationship with you. You are so important that the Creator of the universe is continually advocating for you. He is endlessly paving a way for you to walk into your unique calling and destiny. He is committed to refining you, to training you. He does this because He takes you serious and believes in your potential to step into greatness. All of God's great kingdom stands behind you in support, championing you onward as you understand who you were created to be.

When you are walking in your royal identity as a son or daughter of God, you forcefully advance the kingdom of God wherever you go.

You were created to be a history maker and one who impacts eternity.

This is who you are.

33851711R00075

Made in the USA
San Bernardino, CA
13 May 2016